KLAUS BARBIE

On February 24, 1983, the prosecutor in Lyons, Jean Berthier, read Barbie the following eight charges for which he is scheduled to be tried sometime in 1984. These charges refer to crimes against humanity, for which no statutes of limitation exist.

Killing 22 hostages as a reprisal for an attack upon two German policemen in 1943.

Arrest and torture of 19 people in 1943.

Deportation of 86 people who aided a group of Jews from Lyons.

Execution by firing squad of 42 people among them 40 Jews in and around Lyons during the years 1943/44.

Search and seizure of French railroad workers in 1944 during which two people were killed and several seriously injured as well as others who were never seen again.

Deportation of 650 people, mostly Jews, into the concentration camps of Auschwitz and Ravensbrück. The last transport of this deportation took place on August 11, 1944.

Execution by firing squad of 70 Jews in the town of Bron and several other Jews as well as two clergymen in Saint-Genis-Laval.

Deportation of up to 55 Jews from the village of Izieu, most of whom were children.

As devastating as these charges are, they are by no means all the crimes and atrocities committed by Barbie.

UNCENSORED
EYEWITNESS
ACCOUNT

KLAUS BARBIE

The Shocking Story of How the U.S. Used this Nazi War Criminal as an Intelligence Agent

A First Hand Account by
Erhard Dabringhaus
Barbie's U.S. Intelligence Control Officer

ACROPOLIS BOOKS LTD.
WASHINGTON, D.C.

ACROPOLIS BOOKS LTD.
Colortone Building, 2400 17th St., N.W.,
Washington, D.C. 20009

Printed in the United States of America by
COLORTONE PRESS Creative Graphics, Inc.
Washington, D.C. 20009

Television photographs on pages 16, 17, 18 and 19
courtesy of National Broadcasting Company, Inc., © 1983
by National Broadcasting Company, Inc.

Library of Congress Cataloging in Publication Data

Dabringhaus, Erhard.
    Klaus Barbie: the shocking story of how the U.S.
used this Nazi war criminal as an intelligence agent.

    Includes index.
    1. Military intelligence—United States—History—20th
century.   2. Barbie, Klaus, 1913-   . 3. Dabringhaus,
Erhard.   I. Title
UB251.U5D33 1984   327.1'2'0924   83-27506
ISBN 0-87491-731-X

To:

Gabriel and Daniel
my grandsons.

May they enjoy
freedom and truth in the United States
as their grandfather did.

Contents

Acknowledgments

I wish to thank my immediate family for their encouragement and patience in relinquishing their husband and father to the demands made upon him throughout the year.

Very special thanks are due my very good friend, Helen K. Nielsen, for devoting every free moment of her time to reading and commenting on each page of the manuscript. She was really the first editor of this book.

I also wish to thank Anders O. Kjos for typing and retyping the manuscript. He spent endless hours with me and gave me much support.

In Louvain la Neuve, Belgium, my very good friends, Denise and Marc Roloux, provided me with a base of operations during my European investigations. Denise made valuable comments concerning the initial chapters of the manuscript.

The Spiegel family of Lindau, Germany, deserve my thanks for providing transportation and accommodations during my investigations in Augsburg.

9

I want to thank members of the staff of the newspaper, *Augsburger Allgemeine,* for assistance rendered during my visit. Chief Editor Gernot Römer generously provided documents from the archives. Alfons A. Schertl, editorial staff member, deserves special thanks for providing photos of former U.S. Army installations in Augsburg.

Special thanks to my good friend and colleague Prof. Carl Colditz and his wife Helen for their valuable comments on the manuscript. A very special thanks to Helen Colditz for reading the galley proofs.

Very special thanks are due Bill and Dotty Lucke of Annapolis, Maryland, for introducing me to the president of Acropolis Books Ltd., Alphons J. Hackl, and suggesting the title of the book.

Finally, I must show gratitude to Al Hackl and his editorial staff for their valuable suggestions and persistent encouragement every step of the way.

Introduction

After I revealed on February 5, 1983, that Klaus Barbie was employed by the Army Counter Intelligence Corps (CIC) after World War II, I was inundated by inquiries from all over the world. One week later Barbie was returned to France and people in dozens of countries are now anxiously awaiting his new trial. They hope to learn exactly what Barbie did in France as a war criminal and why the American Army used him, protected him, and then helped him and his family escape to Bolivia.

The furor had died down by midsummer, and as is our custom, my wife and I drove to Annapolis, Maryland, to visit our old American Army friends, Bill and Dotty Lucke, over the Fourth of July weekend. While dining on our favorite Chesapeake Bay blue crabs, Bill suggested that I write a book about my experiences with Barbie. He had followed the Barbie saga with great interest and remarked, "Dabby, there is a publisher in our condo named Al Hackl, who owns Acropolis Books, Ltd. Let's ask him what he thinks of my suggestion."

Al was delighted with the idea and put me under contract. By coincidence it turned out that Alphons J. Hackl and I attended the Military Intelligence Training Center at Camp Ritchie, Maryland, in 1943 at the same time. We also found ourselves on the same plane in September 1943 en route to London as captains of separate Military Intelligence Service teams. Al's name is on my "Short Snorter" dollar bill and is still quite legible after 40 years. During the war, anyone who flew across the ocean was entitled to become a Short Snorter. It was unusual to fly across the ocean in those days, when most soldiers were sent to Europe by troop ship.

In developing this book, I wanted to be certain to tell the true story of the American Intelligence connection. The French connection also had to be handled with special care since Barbie, as the killer of Resistance hero Jean Moulin, is France's most hated Nazi war criminal. There are also some former French collaborators who wish that Barbie had remained in Bolivia.

The Germans, too, want to show their hatred of the Nazi era, and on several recent occasions groups of young Germans demonstrated in front of the house in Augsburg where I had found a safe place for Barbie and his colleague, Kurt Merk.

On my recent visit to Germany I learned how some former German soldiers reacted to the Barbie revelations. One ex-soldier, who had lost his brother in Stalingrad and had barely made it home himself said, "While we poor soldiers had to walk home from the Russian front—hungry, frightened, and abused on the road—you Americans were paying that damn SS Barbie thousands of dollars and putting him up in a warm house!"

Having been an American soldier in Germany at that time, I knew exactly what he was talking about, and he was right!

My report to the media caused our government to investigate Barbie's link to American Intelligence operations. On August 17, 1983, the U.S. Justice Department released its findings in the now famous *Ryan Report*, substantiating each of my previous allegations. The U.S. even saw fit to send an apology to France, stating, "Justice delayed is Justice denied."

Few other countries would have made this admission, but in a democracy, the truth should prevail. This is the reason for my book. Because some of the truth about the Barbie episode has been hidden, veiled, or omitted in the *Ryan Report*, here is an eye-witness account, which examines these omissions and contradictions so that the U.S. involvement with the infamous "Butcher of Lyons" can be seen in a clearer light.

The following account of my dealings with Barbie in 1948 will reveal the kind of man he really is, as well as how he turned from Nazi enforcer to U.S. informant.

1 The Shock Of Recognition

"Good Lord, Jenny, look!"
It was an ordinary evening, a Saturday evening, and my wife Jenny and I were having supper in our Grosse Pointe, Michigan home. The TV set was on in the background, and we had been listening to the evening news. The program, we were to recall later, was NBC's weekend edition of the "Nightly News." The date was Saturday, January 29, 1983.

The names in the news were the familiar mixture of celebrities—political bigwigs, sports stars, film personalities—and anonymous bystanders caught up in the day's happenings. Among the distant cities in the spotlight that night was La Paz, Bolivia.

Suddenly, as anchorwoman Jessica Savitch described the predicament of a jailed Bolivian businessman, she spoke the name of a man who had played an unforgettable role in my past. I spun around to face the screen, and the shock of recognition hit me with a force that jolted me back 35 years. As I stared in disbelief, I realized that before me, alive and well, was the infamous Nazi Klaus Barbie—the loathsome "Butcher of Lyons." We listened in stunned silence as Savitch commented on the scene in La Paz:

15

Saturday, January 29, 1983, NBC "Nightly News"

From La Paz, Bolivia
Klaus Altmann (Klaus Barbie) . . .

A peaceful scene of the city of La Paz, Bolivia

*Restaurant where Klaus Barbie met with his cronies on a regular basis —
sitting in the corner so that he could observe all entrances . . .*

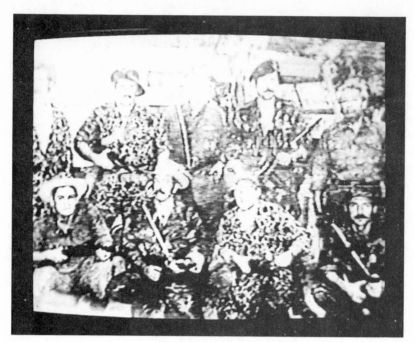

Some of Barbie's "friends" in Bolivia

Barbie with his bodyguard

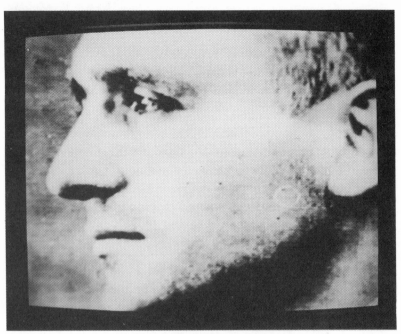

Profile of Barbie in the forties

Barbie now, after having been arrested in La Paz enroute to courthouse

Chilled, I turned to Jenny and said, "That is the s.o.b. who worked for me in Germany, in 1948, when I was a special agent for the U.S. Counter Intelligence Corps in Augsburg."

The round face was unmistakable. The narrow, beady blue eyes gazed calmly into the camera. There, seated in a jail cell in faraway Bolivia, was the stocky figure of one of Hitler's most murderous officers, who, when asked about the atrocities he had committed during the occupation of France, had sworn he would repeat them a thousand times over.

As "Klaus Altmann," Barbie had reportedly lived in Bolivia for many years. I had seen photographs of Altmann/Barbie before, but they had been blurred, or taken at odd angles, or shot from long distances. This time there was no question. These were indeed the familiar features of the man who had worked for me as a well-paid informant for American counterintelligence. In fact, Barbie actually spent more time working for the Americans as an intelligence agent—from April 1947 to March 1951—than he did for Hitler.

Barbie had not lost his authoritative air; it had no doubt served him well in his transition to Bolivian business execu- tive. He looked quite unconcerned. A colleague was report- edly on his way to settle accounts with the Bolivian State Mining Company, after which he was to be freed.

But, I wondered, would he be freed if the general public realized the full extent of his crimes? And how had he been able to avoid the French authorities for so many years? Was it true that their search had been less than diligent out of fear of embarrassing Barbie's one-time collaborators? What about the mysterious death of his co-worker, Kurt Merk—could Merk have known too much about how Barbie carried out his "duties"?

Among the questions whirling in my thoughts, one kept coming to the fore: *should the world be told that Barbie— after having committed his monstrous atrocities—had been put on the official payroll of the United States Government?*

Almost no one, it seemed, outside of the CIC, knew that he had actively worked for the U.S. As a professor of German Language and Literature at Detroit's Wayne State University, I was often invited by the Consul General of the Federal Republic of Germany to parties commemorating the founding of the new Federal Republic. These events were often attended by the French Counsul. On a number of occasions after Barbie's name had appeared in the media, I mentioned to the French Consul what I knew about Barbie's employment by the U.S.

To my surprise, the response was always "He is out of our reach—there is no extradition treaty between France and Bolivia. Our hands are tied."

But now the public had been told who—and where—the real Klaus Barbie was. Was it also time for them to know of his U.S. connection?

I decided that my answer had to be yes. Jenny, who as a war bride had experienced four years of German occupation in her native Belgium, was quick to agree. Thus a chain of events was set in motion that was to dramatically change my life and, I hoped, that of Klaus Barbie.

Disclosure time: I contact NBC

The January 29th newscast invoked vivid memories of Europe in the late '40's. As I explained to Jenny, 'When we lived in Augsburg in 1948, the network of informants for which I was control officer included Barbie. Do you remember when I was dressed like a German, in a suit made by a local tailor, and carried a German identification card?

"Klaus Barbie's associate at that time was a former German Intelligence officer named Kurt Merk, who was regular German army, not SS. Those two were the top operatives of a network of informants which had the code name "Petersen Network" employed by our intelligence unit. I was given the job of taking over the network, translating all of the information, and passing it on to our headquarters in Munich. I think I have to tell the world this notorious Nazi once worked for the United States Government."

Over the weekend I considered various ways in which I might accomplish this. On Monday morning I wrote a letter to NBC Network News in New York, telling them some of what I remembered about Klaus Barbie. There was as yet no guarantee that Barbie would be returned to France, and I wondered if greater public interest in his criminal career would affect Bolivia's reluctance to release him.

Director, NBC News   January 31, 1983
30 Rockefeller Plaza
New York, NY 10020

Gentlemen:

Several recent news items regarding a former German Nazi criminal have appeared on your Nightly News broadcasts (Saturday, January 29, 1983, with Jessica Savitch as commentator), and have prompted me to write to you in order to add some pertinent additional information. The subject is Klaus Barbie—alias Klaus Altmann—whom I was able to recognize in your news broadcast.

I was a member of the U.S. Counter Intelligence Corps (CIC) in 1948, stationed in Augsburg,

Germany, where I first met Klaus Barbie and worked with him for nearly a year as the head of an information network that he had organized and offered to the American Intelligence community for a price. His associate was a man named Kurt Merk, a former member of the regular German Army Intelligence organization, stationed in France throughout several years of German occupation. Both men were totally familiar with each other's work in France, and contrary to many recent news reports, Barbie was not a member of the Gestapo, but a member of the SD *(Sicherheitsdienst—* Security Service or Counter Intelligence.) His prime area of operation was between Lyons and Besançon.

Upon orders from our own American Intelligence Service in Frankfurt, I was asked to bring Klaus Barbie and Kurt Merk from the town of Memmingen to Augsburg, where my CIC unit was stationed. After providing proper housing for these two men and some of their friends, I met with both of them at least three times a week to edit information which they provided, and I then forwarded this report to our higher headquarters. For this service I was authorized to pay $1,700 per month in American dollars, which the two men ostensibly divided among their informants in the field.

On two separate occasions French Intelligence agents requested to talk to me in regards to the whereabouts of Klaus Barbie. A French Resistance Officer by the name of Colonel Hardy was being tried in Paris for collaboration. Klaus Barbie had captured Colonel Hardy on a train and for several weeks had tried to make him work for German Intelligence. According to Barbie, the Colonel never broke during interrogation, never collaborated, and eventually was able to escape; the French government misconstrued the escape as a release.

Upon instructions from my own higher
headquarters, I was told to deny to the French
agents that I knew where Klaus Barbie was; in fact,
I convinced them, "I never even heard of the man."
Personally, I was very upset that I could not turn
him over to the French at the time. I later learned
from Kurt Merk that he actually deserved the title
of "Butcher of Lyons," having killed over 200
French throughout the period of their association in
France.

It appeared to me at that time that whenever the
two men had an argument over the distribution of
the American dollars that I paid them, they told me
stories about each other that focused on the
atrocities committed by each of the men in France.
At one time Kurt Merk remarked that the SD in
France had more power than the German Military
Commander; and if the French ever found all the
mass graves that Klaus Barbie was responsible for,
even General Eisenhower could not prevent his
being turned over to the French for war crimes
committed by him.

It appears that Klaus Barbie was able to save
enough of the money paid him to obtain
transportation to South America in 1951, thus
eluding further prosecution.

If Klaus Barbie is ever brought to trial in France
or West Germany, I would be willing to testify,
since I recall many more crimes committed by
Barbie in France during the occupation. I hope this
information will be given to the proper people, to
bring this war criminal to his deserved end.

Sincerely,

Erhard Dabringhaus

Erhard Dabringhaus

NBC News interviews me; Barbie spirited
out of Bolivia

I mailed my letter on Monday and heard nothing until the following Saturday. On February 5, 1983, as I walked into my house, the phone was ringing. A man from Chicago introduced himself as Mr. Prince, the midwest representative of NBC News. He had been called out of bed early that morning and told to get in touch with me. Someone in New York had finally read my letter. "Mr. Dabringhaus," he said, "we've been trying all morning to get you. I wonder if you would possibly consider giving our people an interview regarding your association with Klaus Barbie?"

"Since I wrote you a letter, I'm willing to be interviewed about him," I replied.

Prince continued, "We have a young man in an airplane right now coming from Chicago. He should land at Detroit City Airport by two o'clock. He will pick up a camera crew and a sound man. If it's all right with you, they should be at your house by 2:30."

A very pleasant young man, Barry Hohlfelder, arrived at the appointed time with a cameraman and two technicians. By three o'clock they had my living room turned into a TV studio. They moved furniture, put lights in the proper corners, and sat me on a sofa.

Suddenly, Hohlfelder asked, "How do we know that you really did work for the CIC in 1948?" As it dawned on me that I could have been some eccentric telling a phoney story, I hurriedly dug up some old records and went through photo albums from that period of my stay in Germany. I found a registration card permitting me to keep a gun in my living quarters. It was a permit dated April, 1948, signed by the Provost Marshall of the city of Augsburg, identifying me as a member of the 970th CIC detachment.

                                    HEADQUARTERS
                                970th CIC DETACHMENT
                            REGION IV, APO 407-A, US ARMY
                                AUGSBURG SUB-REGION

                                                    28 April 1948

                            AFFIDAVIT

1. This is to certify that the following described pistol has been registered as a war trophy and has been in my possession since August 1944.

      Name & Make: Walther
      Model: PPK
      Caliber: 7.65 mm
      Type: Semi-Automatic
      Number: 833427
      Description: Brown plastic handle and the name F.GUNTHER, Wiesbaden is carved in grip.

2. I acquired this pistol during the war as a Captain with the 1st US Inf.Division. In France I took German Hauptmann Gunther Prisoner myself and have since that time kept the pistol as a war trophy.

3. It has been at the home of my wife in Liege, Belgium since it was registered as a trophy.

4. I swear that the above information is true and correct.

5. I am 31 years of age, 5'9" Height, 180 lbs Weight, blue-grey eyes, light brown hair.

                                    ERHARD DABRINGHAUS
                                    S/A   CIC

With this in hand, the interview began and I was on camera.

The filming ended at approximately 3:30 p.m., and to my astonishment, the same national news program I had watched the previous Saturday had *my* story on the air shortly after 6:30 p.m. that evening. Before the NBC crew left, my living room was restored to its original order. Not a single piece of furniture was out of place.

At 10:00 a.m. on Sunday, the telephone began ringing non-stop. The information that had been aired on Saturday caused considerable consternation and made many people uneasy. They just couldn't believe what they had heard. A few days later, I would also start receiving hate-mail from such groups as the Detroit Nazis and the White People's

Party; an example is reproduced below. Threatening phone calls intensified to such a point that the university felt it necessary to provide me with police protection in the classroom and around the clock at my home.

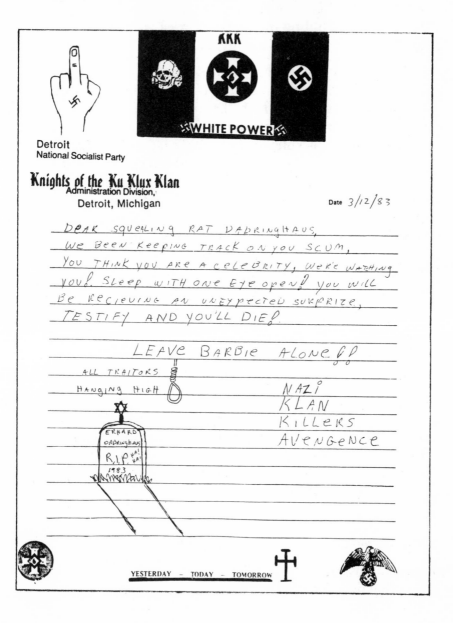

It was not generally known that the United States had employed Nazi war criminals as informants. From his jail cell in faraway Bolivia, Klaus Barbie had drawn the attention of the world. Although it had been occasionally reported during the last 30 years that he was among the Nazi fugitives hiding in South America, he had prospered and lived a free life as a Bolivian citizen.

The most unbelievable coincidence (or was it purely coincidence?), which gave my story international prominence, was the fact that while NBC News was interviewing me on February 5, it was announced that Barbie had been spirited out of his jail cell in La Paz, Bolivia. He had been sent by plane to French Guiana, where a French military aircraft was waiting. By the time my interview with NBC was aired, Klaus Barbie was back in France. This was an incredible set of circumstances—no one expected that Bolivia would return Barbie to France. Several earlier attempts to extradite him had failed. Both West Germany and France had requested extradition in recent years, but there had been no indication of compliance by Bolivia, which had never before honored extradition requests.

It was recently rumored that President Mitterrand had offered Bolivia considerable economic help in return for Barbie.

Barbie's defense lawyer, Jacques Verges has frequently implied that Barbie was the victim of a secret deal made between France and Bolivia. A gift of 13 million dollars and 3,360 tons of wheat helped expel Barbie from Bolivia and brought him to France.

The Barbie story explodes in the media

On Sunday, February 6, 1983, a line of reporters formed at my front door. They continued to write for three weeks, and

The author with a Nazi dagger. Photo by the author's daughter, Greta.

calls came in from as far away as Sidney, Australia. Our local *Detroit News* staff writer Lowell Cauffiel taped a lengthy interview. He and cameraman Edward C. Lombardo insisted on taking a picture of me sitting at my desk in my study. On the desk was a Nazi dagger which I have used for 35 years as a letter opener. In order to tie the 50-year-old Nazi era with Barbie and me, he asked me to hold the dagger in one hand and to place my right hand on a volume of Herman Wouk's Winds of War, which was to begin that night as an ABC mini-series.

The appearance of my story in conjunction with this chronicle of the events World War II initiated a tremendous uproar, the effects of which are likely to be felt for many years.

The scene of Barbie's crimes and atrocities—The Prison Militaire, Ft. Montluc, Lyons to which Barbie has returned symbolically, before being transferred to the more secure St. Joseph Prison, Lyons, where he is now awaiting his trial.

Another view of Ft. Montluc, where Barbie tortured and killed his victims.

The Klarsfeld connection

I must point out here that Serge and Beate Klarsfeld worked tirelessly to bring Barbie to justice. Klarsfeld is a French attorney and his wife is from Germany. For more than 11 years they tracked Barbie through various hiding places in South America and made every effort to convince West German and French authorities that Klaus Altmann and Klaus Barbie were one and the same: the wanted Nazi fugitive. At one point Germany had closed its files on Barbie and it appeared that France was losing interest in the search. The Butcher of Lyons was, meanwhile, becoming firmly entrenched in Bolivia, seemingly out of reach.

The procedure used to transfer Barbie from Bolivian to French jurisdiction was highly irregular. He was not really extradited, but simply expelled as an undesirable naturalized citizen who had obtained his Bolivian nationality fraudulently by using a false name and false documents. It is customary to offer an expelled person the right to choose a country which is willing to accept him. Bolivia's Minister of the Interior maintained that France was the only country in Europe willing to accept Barbie. Yet if Bolivia revoked Barbie's citizenship because it had been obtained through false statements, he would presumably again be a German citizen and Germany would also accept him. Besides, they had already requested his extradition. Finally, Barbie didn't have to go to a European country. The Bolivian government simply made a political decision, disdaining official channels and diplomatic niceties.

Swathed in a blanket to hide his identity, Barbie was placed on an airplane with the explanation that he was being sent into exile in Paraguay, a decision that he would have accepted without argument. Instead the plane landed in French Guiana, where a military DC 8, heavily guarded by French agents and military personnel, was waiting to

*Rear view of St. Joseph Prison, Lyons, where Barbie is carefully
guarded night and day to insure that nothing happens to him and that
he will be available for the trial.*

*The Palace of Justice in Lyons where the trial of Klaus Barbie is
expected to take place*

dispatch him to the scene of his crimes. When Barbie realized that he was in the hands of the French, one onlooker remarked that his jaw dropped nearly to his chest. The decades of deception were over.

His dismay at finding himself in French custody is graphically illustrated by France's official indictment.

On February 24, 1983, the prosecutor in Lyons, Jean Berthier, read Barbie the following eight charges for which he is scheduled to be tried sometime in 1984. These charges refer to crimes against humanity, for which no statutes of limitation exist.

1. **Killing 22 hostages as a reprisal for an attack upon two German policemen in 1943.**

2. **Arrest and torture of 19 people in 1943.**

3. **Deportation of 86 people who aided a group of Jews from Lyons.**

4. **Execution by firing squad of 42 people among them 40 Jews in and around Lyons during the years 1943/44.**

5. **Search and seizure of French railroad workers in 1944 during which two people were killed and several seriously injured as well as others who were never seen again.**

6. **Deportation of 650 people, mostly Jews, into the concentration camps of Auschwitz and Ravensbrück. The last transport of this deportation took place on August 11, 1944.**

7. **Execution by firing squad of 70 Jews in the town of Bron and several other Jews as well as two clergymen in Saint-Genis-Laval.**

8. **Deportation of up to 55 Jews from the village of Izieu, most of whom were children.**

As devastating as these charges are, they are by no means all the crimes and atrocities committed by Barbie.

But the prosecutor did not read Barbie the list of crimes he had committed in Lyons, for which he had earlier been tried in absentia, as he cannot be tried for them again.

Barbie was a diehard Nazi—loyal, brutal, but not terribly bright. He had been an indifferent student, graduating from high school two years behind his class.

The memories that Klaus Barbie evokes are totally repugnant. He was a true Nazi sadist. He would fondle one woman on his knees as he ordered another alternately beaten and dunked in ice water. When he tired of his Swiss mistress, Heidi, he shot her.

He was the prototype of the SS strong man, strutting about with his shirt sleeves rolled up, snapping his riding crop. He often carried a club, sometimes a simple two-by-four, with which to beat his prisoners. He once snatched a Jewish baby from its mother's arms and tossed it on a train to Auschwitz. One of his most horrifying acts of reprisal was to lock 100 children in a schoolhouse, which he then burned and dynamited. Barbie's record, a model of Hitler's savagery, earned him numerous decorations.

As Germany's SD intelligence Chief in Lyons from 1942 to 1944, he personally had a hand in 4,342 murders and saw to it that nearly 8,000 people were shipped to death camps. These are the numbers arrived at by the French courts that twice sentenced him to death—in 1952 and again in 1954. During an interview in Bolivia in 1978, he was completely unrepentant. "What is there to regret? I'm a committed Nazi and if I had to be born a thousand times over I would be a thousand times what I have been." He once claimed to have found ammunition in a convent, which was all the reason he needed to murder each of the nuns by firing squad. Barbie would also use French "Miliz" soldiers, recruited mostly from French Vichy collaborators, to shoot and kill French Maquis freedom fighters to test their loyalty to the Nazis. Before giving the Miliz this assignment, he usually made them first change into German *Wehrmacht* uniforms.

This was his method of insuring an adequate supply of French collaborators and traitors. In order to prove their loyalty they were forced to participate in attacks against Resistance fighters, during which they had to shoot their own countrymen. Whenever he observed a collaborator aiming away from a French target, he would avenge this disloyalty by shooting him on the spot.

Whenever someone refused to admit to membership in the Resistance, or if a prisoner escaped, he would order hostages taken and immediately shot. One of his favorite tricks was to leave the cell doors of a prison block unlocked and to place several machine guns strategically near the outside doors of the prison. During air raid alarms, the prisoners would try to escape, hoping that the German soldiers had taken cover. The moment the prisoners got outside, the machine guns would open fire and dozens of prisoners would be cut to ribbons on the street. Barbie is said to have stated, "You know, I really don't believe the story about gassing six million Jews, but I regret every Jew that I did not eliminate."

One of the most important questions Barbie will face during the trial will be who betrayed Jean Moulin. Prosecutors are likely to question him exhaustively about that fateful afternoon when seven leaders of the Resistance were arrested by Barbie's commandos in the house of a doctor in Caluire, a suburb of Lyons. Barbie has said that he was led to the meeting place by a traitor who marked the route with chalk marks. It has long been known, however, that the captured Moulin was so savagely beaten and tortured by Barbie in his SD headquarters at Avenue Barthelot 14 that he died shortly thereafter.

Eyewitness Gottlieb Fuchs, at that time a translator for Barbie, now lives in Switzerland. He says: "I was there when Barbie beat Moulin with a club to his head and body; after he had fallen to the floor, he kicked him with his boots.

He then dragged him by his feet down a cellar staircase and left him lying there. When Barbie came back up I literally heard him say, 'If that dog has not croaked by tomorrow, then I will finish him off myself.'"

2 The Beginning Of U.S./U.S.S.R. Friction

The need for German intelligence know-how sets stage for Barbie's emergence as U.S. informant

To place the Barbie affair in perspective, it is necessary to examine the period immediately after World War II.

The United States had helped the Russian Army, through such cooperative efforts as the lend-lease program, which provided both equipment and know-how, to withstand the German onslaught. Many believed that this assistance from the western world might encourage the Russians to change their totalitarian communist tune and become more democratic. Soon after the war ended, these hopes faded in the face of the Russians' display of total disregard for human life. The distrust between Western Allies and Russia became known throughout Europe immediately upon the cessation of hostilities.

The Germans wanted to sign an unconditional surrender with the Western Allies. U.S. General Dwight D. Eisenhower, at his headquarters in Reims, had prepared for this surrender ceremony, but the Russians were not satisfied with his plans. They believed that the U.S. and its allies were making a separate peace with the Germans and insisted that the final surrender document be signed in Berlin, the capital of the aggressor nation.

All of the necessary signatures had been obtained in Reims on May 7, 1945. But Russian General Ivan Susloparov, liaison officer at Allied Headquarters, had signed without Moscow's consent. Eisenhower agreed to sign the document the following day, May 8, 1945 in Berlin, with Marshall Zhukov, the representative of the Soviet Military on hand, as a favor to the Russians.

Thus it appeared that not one but two World Wars had ended: one, between Germany and the Western Allies, with the surrender document signed in Reims, and the other between Germany and the Russians, with the surrender document signed in Berlin.

Concessions to Russians compromise U.S. position

Eisenhower's famous decision not to press on to take Berlin was probably not his to make. The arrangements to allow the Soviet Union to enter Berlin first grew out of the London Agreement of September 1944. Stalin had demanded the strongest assurances from Roosevelt and Churchill that the conquest of the capital of Nazism be reserved for the Russians.

In return for letting the Russians take Berlin, we had obtained Soviet agreement to join the United Nations, which was to be formed immediately after the war. If the Western Allies had entered Berlin before the Russians, the entire show that the Soviets had planned for the final surrender ceremony would have been upset.

Europe

Map Courtesy Central Intelligence Agency

Events Leading Up To

January 30, 1933
Adolf Hitler appointed Chancellor of Germany.

October 25, 1936
Formation of the Berlin-Rome Axis.

August 23-24, 1939
The Soviet-German Nonaggression Pact is signed in Moscow.

September 1, 1939
World War II begins, Germany invades Poland.

September 29, 1939
A Soviet-German Friendship Treaty is signed.

February 21, 1940
The Russian-Finnish war with heavy Russian losses suggests to the Allied and Axis observers that Stalin's officer purges have weakened his army. This impression of weakness contributes to Hitler's decision to invade the USSR and makes the British and Americans reluctant to help the Soviets. Everyone believes the Germans will win quickly when they invade.

May 29-June 3, 1940
British forces withdrawan from Dunkirk.

June 14, 1940
German troops occupy Paris. Marshal Henri Pétain becomes head of French government.

June 22, 1940
France surrenders to Germany. Vichy in Southern France becomes provisional capital. Lyon would be the largest city of unoccupied France where Barbie also would set up headquarters for his S.D. (Nazi SS Security Service).

July 10, 1940
Death of the 3rd Republic. Laval and Pétain take over. Referred to as Vichy Government from then on.

October 11, 1940
Pétain broadcasts to the French people advocating support for Germany.

October 28, 1940
Laval becomes Foreign Minister of the Vichy government.

June 22, 1941
Operation Barbarossa: the German attack on the Soviet Union begins. The Soviet forces are taken by surprise and losses are very heavy in the first encounters.

July 11, 1941
Roosevelt appoints William Donovan to head a new civilian intelligence agency, the Office for Strategic Services (OSS).

July 12, 1941
Britian and the Soviet Union sign a mutual assistance agreement. It forbids making a separate peace.

August 2, 1941
The Soviet Union begins to receive U.S. Lend-Lease aid.

August 9-12, 1941
The Atlantic Charter agreement—a statement of the principles governing the war policies of Britain and America.

September 6, 1941
Heydrich, head of the security services (SD, a division of the SS), orders all Jews over the age of six to wear a distinguishing Star of David badge.

September 24, 1941
The Atlantic Charter is signed by 15 governments.

October 1, 1941
By joint declaration Britain and America continue sending and increasing the extent of help to the Soviet Union.

November 17, 1941
Rosenberg, the Nazi "racial expert," is appointed as head of a new Reich Ministry for Occupied Eastern Territories. His task is to exploit the Baltic states and White Russia for German economic benefit and to rid them of "undesirable elements" such as Jews, Gypsies, and Communist supporters. Five extermination camps, Auschwitz, Chelmno, Treblinka, Sobibor, and Belsec are established: their mission is to kill. Separate concentration camps are set up to work their inmates to death amid filthy conditions and starvation rations.

U.S./U.S.S.R. Friction

December 7, 1941
Japaneese forces attack Pearl Harbor.

January 20, 1942
At the Wannsee Conference in Berlin, Heydrich offers plans to Hitler for the "Final Solution" to the "Jewish Problem."

January 14-24, 1943
Churchill and Roosevelt meet in Casablanca and agree on unconditional surrender terms for the Axis.

August 13-24, 1943
The Quebec Conference of British and American military leaders, joined by Roosevelt and Churchill, discusses the invasion of Europe.

November 28-December 1, 1943
Roosevelt, Churchill, and Stalin and their staffs meet at Teheran to agree on war plans. Security problems exist and there are suspicions that the Americans' accommodations are bugged. The Americans are cautious not to appear pro-British and anti-Soviet Union. This stance causes them to make too many concessions.

September 1944
London Agreement. Meeting of Allied Chiefs of Staff. Stalin extracts from Roosevelt the assurance that the conquest of Berlin will be reserved for the Russians.

February 4-11, 1945
Roosevelt, Churchill, and Stalin, and their senior military and political colleagues meet at Yalta in the Crimea. The war in Europe is nearly won. Britain and the U.S. believe that much has to be done to defeat Japan. Roosevelt's illness seems to be weakening his negotiating powers and judgment. This contributes to Stalin obtaining the promise of territorial concessions in Sakhalin and the Kurile Islands in return for a promise to declare war on Japan. Arrangements for the division of Germany into occupation zones for each of the major powers are confirmed and defined. Repatriation of Soviet citizens is agreed upon. Establishment of a United Nations Organization is discussed; the first meetings are scheduled for April in San Francisco.

April 30, 1945
Hitler and Eva Braun commit suicide in Hitler's Bunker at 15:30 hours. Their bodies are cremated with gasoline.

May 8, 1945
The British and Americans celebrate VE (Victory in Europe) Day.

July 17-August 2, 1945
Truman, Stalin, and Churchill meet at Potsdam. On July 24, Truman and Churchill tell Stalin that they possess a new and powerful weapon for use against Japan but do not elaborate.

March 1946
In Fulton, Missouri, Churchill delivers a public speech in the presence of President Truman in which he describes how an "Iron Curtain has descended across Europe."

March 31, 1948
Marshall Plan. Congress passes the Foreign Assistance Act allocating $5,300,000,000 for aid to Europe.

July 24, 1948
The Berlin blockade begins after disagreements over currency reform. The Soviets close the access routes to Berlin. The Western powers decide to airlift supplies into Berlin as a temporary measure. The airlift proves so successful that it continues until the blockade ends in September 1949.

August 12, 1945
VJ (Victory in Japan) Day.

September 1948
A Parliamentary Council meets in Bonn to draw up a constitution for West Germany as a new independent country. It is completed in April 1949; in August 1949, the first elections install Konrad Adenauer as Chancellor.

August 1949
The Soviet Union explodes its first atomic weapon, bringing the American monopoly to an end.

The relationship between the Western Allies and the Soviet Union cannot be identified as a true alliance. Rather, it was dictated by the fact that both sides wanted to eliminate the tyranny of Nazism; it was simply a liaison based on mutual assistance. As soon as the war was over, the Russians once again began to play their deceitful game.

Yalta Agreement forces repatriation of unwilling Soviets

The Yalta Conference of early 1945 contributed more to chaotic conditions in post-war Europe than any previous agreements between Russia and the West had done. One of its underlying decrees, which was signed by Stalin, Roosevelt, and Churchill, demanded the total repatriation of all Soviet citizens after the war, irrespective of their individual wishes and, if necessary, by force.

How could representatives of free nations have signed such a document? Today we know that American and British soldiers were required to participate in the forced repatriation of Soviet forced laborers and Soviet soldiers. It was known even then that we were sending them to death or to a lifetime of servitude.

It is inappropriate and melodramatic to compare American Army officers engaged in sending Russian citizens to their death and Barbie sitting in a prison in Lyons, France, awaiting trial for similar crimes. Barbie has never shown remorse, but Americans frequently voice their regret for Hiroshima and the fire-bombing of Dresden.

German military warns of Soviet aims

The defeated German army returning from the Eastern front clearly knew the Russians better than we did. Once a German commander surrendered his troops and equipment intact to us stating, "Let's turn around and go to Moscow together. All we need is gas and food. Sooner or later you're going to have to fight them anyway because they cannot be trusted." When the First U.S. Infantry Division accepted the final surrender of German troops facing the Americans in Czechoslovakia, I immediately recognized Germany's fear of and respect for Russia.

On May 9, 1945, General George Taylor, Assistant Division Commander of the First Infantry Division, accepted the final surrender from Germany's General Theodor Osterkamp. The ceremony took place in Ellbogen, Czechoslovakia, in a small tavern called *"Zum Weissen Ross"* (The White Horse Inn). General Osterkamp came to the meeting prepared to sign the surrender document. He was asked how many troops he still had under his command. His Chief of Staff gave him the final morning report and stated that they were in command of some 18,000 German troops. The troops were sent to an airfield that was hurriedly prepared as a prisoner-of-war enclosure. The former German military airfield, located just outside the Czechoslovakian town of Cheb (Eger), was approximately three miles long and two miles wide.

During the ceremonies at the tavern, General Osterkamp tried to stall for time. He asked whether the dateline Ellbogen, Czechoslovakia, was not in error. "To my knowledge," General Osterkamp said, "This is Ellbogen, Sudetenland."

I translated the General's concern to General Taylor, who flushed from his collar on up and shouted, "You tell him that there is no such God damned place as Sudetenland! We are here in Czechoslovakia and that's the way the document will read."

I translated General Taylor's words into idiomatic German to retain their flavor. General Osterkamp immediately picked up the pen, signed the document, and the ceremonies were over.

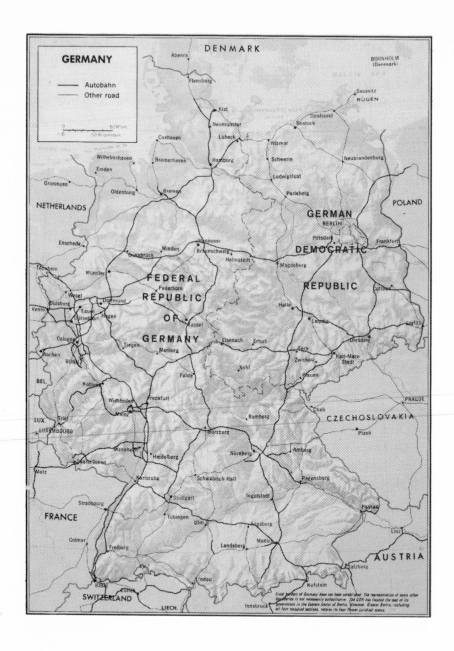

Map Courtesy Central Intelligence Agency

German prisoners flock to U.S. camp

After we had turned the German military airfield into a prisoner of war enclosure, our own Brigadier General William E. Waters, Division Artillery Commander, was put in charge of overall administration. It was my job to interrogate incoming prisoners so they could be discharged and sent home as soon as possible. After the first 18,000 German troops under the command of General Osterkamp arrived, we noticed that the total number of prisoners was growing larger and larger. By May 15, there were more than 25,000 in the airfield. We were not prepared for this and didn't understand where they had all come from.

All the Germans who had fled from the Eastern front were trapped in a no man's land between the American and Russian line. Their objective was to get into the hands of the American Army as quickly as possible. By the end of the second week, the enclosure contained 50,000 troops. One week later the total had reached 100,000. In order to get some semblance of order, we asked German officers to organize the entire group and they methodically arranged the prisoners into groups of one hundred each.

How were all these people getting there? They used every conceivable means of transporation to get to the Cheb airfield. There were whole convoys of German troops, women, and children—everybody was coming to the American line, in wheelbarrows, tremendous army troop transports, civilian buses, pushcarts, horses and wagons, sporty civilian cars, general staff cars, bicycles and buggies—anything to transport them away from the Russian line. When the number of Germans in the airfield reached 125,000, the pressure was enormous.

I remember the day when we abruptly received orders to accept no more German prisoners. We had to face them about and send them off toward the Russian line. This, too, was part of the Yalta agreement. Only those troops fighting the West should become prisoners of the West, and those fighting the East should become prisoners of the Russians.

General Waters ordered machine guns placed on the roads leading into the prisoner of war enclosure. In order to show that we were serious, we fired several machine-gun bursts over the heads of people trying to get in. It was a horrifying sight to see some of the German soldiers take their pistols and blow their brains out rather than become prisoners of the Russians. This was perhaps the first time in history when machine guns were used to keep prisoners from getting in rather than getting out.

American combat officers certainly saw what kind of power politics the Russians were playing. It would have been to our advantage in 1945 to tell the Russians to go to hell. Unfortunately, we were too busy basking in the glory of our victory to distinguish between two brutal systems of dictatorship. The Soviet fear that a common cause was developing between the Western Allies and the Germans was based on a Communist theory that a natural affinity exists between capitalism and fascism.

U.S. troops returned prematurely

America redeployed its combat troops back to the states too rapidly after the war. The new arrivals did not have combat experience and lacked firsthand knowledge of what the Russians and Germans had done during the war. We were bragging about having beaten the so-called best soldiers in the world, the Prussian Army. We forgot to tell them about the atrocities on both sides. The men who hired Barbie and worked with him had not seen these atrocities and had not learned that we repatriated Russians at the point of a bayonet. They quickly learned, however, that the Russians had not changed. Consequently, they hired men like Barbie and other SS officers to fight against them. A well-defined national policy vis-a-vis the Russians did not exist.

3   Who hired Klaus Barbie?

Recovery seeds sown

By 1947, the United States had occupied the American Zone of Germany for two years. U.S. combat troops had done an admirable job of bringing order to chaos and sowing the seeds of recovery. After these combat troops were redeployed to the States, their inexperienced replacements made many mistakes. The military government organized in Washington and the officer training schools taught neither the language nor the basic cultural history of Germany. A colonel in charge of the city of Ansbach told me that the extent of his university training was what kind of trees grow in Bavaria, which qualified him as a military affairs officer in occupied Germany.

Rebuilding Germany's cigarette-butt economy

Germany became a cigarette-butt economy on May 8, 1945. When G.I.'s entered a conference room or emerged from a movie, there were always at least 10 or 15 young German kids waiting outside. They followed us as we smoked. As we

49

flipped our cigarette butts into the gutters, at least a dozen kids would dive for them. With three butts, you could roll a new cigarette. They took the butts home to their parents or made new cigarettes to barter for food.

Germany was truly down and out. Her cities were destroyed and nearly every house was damaged. American G.I.'s helped out. Our soldiers were generous with their PX rations, chocolate bars, and cigarettes. For the Germans, broken and shattered, the only way to go was up. Traditional German industriousness had to be rekindled, but it was not going to be easy; estimates of the time needed to rebuild Germany ranged from 20 to 30 years.

But they were wrong. The economic miracle began soon after the war. In June of 1948, a monetary change was carried out; the old Reichsmark was replaced by the Deutsche Mark (DM). Chancellor Konrad Adenauer and Finance Minister Ludwig Erhard, aided by the American Marshall Plan, helped to create the economic miracle of Germany's recovery.

The reconstruction and the rebuilding of German cities was begun by their women. As I drove through the various destroyed towns, I could see women of all ages, hammer in hand, knocking mortar off old bricks and stacking them in tidy square piles. Few of their men had yet returned but the rebuilding of Germany was under way.

Postwar culture shock

The war brought about an enormous change in Germany's strict pre-war social mores. Although their need for food and shelter was an important factor, the nightmare of Hitlerism and the loss of the war had the greatest cultural impact on the minds and hearts of the people. Most Germans had been convinced by Hitler that their army was invincible. But Hitler was wrong!

The barter system took many forms. A family in Augsburg obtained their supplies by giving their bedroom to their 18-year-old daughter so that she could entertain her American boyfriend in private. Mother and father slept on mattresses on the kitchen floor. Before the G.I. could enter the bedroom, he had to put his bag of PX rations on the kitchen table.

Germans began to denounce one another. None of them, of course, had ever been Nazis, but the man across the street, he was a big Nazi. Thus went the explanations as we searched private homes for documents and weapons. These denunciations were daily occurrences. When interrogated, the Germans routinely asserted that they were only small fish in the pond. "I just went along with the crowd. I never participated in anything other than to march along like the rest of them." The German word for that kind of person is *Mitläufer*—someone who just "follows along."

Merk hired in 1946

During this turmoil, CIC was the largest American intelligence organization in occupied Germany. Trying to establish order and justice in this chaotic setting was an enormous task.

Lt. Colonel Dale Garvey was Commander of Region IV of the 970th CIC Detachment in Munich. Robert S. Taylor was one of his agents. Agent Taylor had used Kurt Merk as a paid informant in Memmingen since 1946. Merk, an *Abwehr* (Military Intelligence) officer, had served in Dijon and Paris during the war.

Merk's qualifications as an intelligence agent were revealed when he was first interrogated. Agent Taylor immediately recognized the value of Merk's cooperation; he could reestablish the network of informants that had functioned admirably during the war. And because he was not

SS—just regular army—atrocities did not weigh heavily
against his background. Although his rank of captain in the
German Intelligence Service required his arrest, this could
easily be circumvented by reporting that he had been thoroughly interrogated and no incriminating information
found.

Merk had returned with his mistress from France,
where she had been instrumental in helping him penetrate
French resistance organizations. Because she was wanted
by the French as a collaborator, he sought the security of
the American Army in order to protect her.

Barbie joins Merk to help lead Petersen Network

In April of 1947 Merk met Klaus Barbie at a railroad
station. They had known each other in France, where they
had worked in the same area. Merk immediately offered
Barbie a job with the Americans. When this proposition
was presented to Colonel Garvey, he was more than happy
to accept, providing Barbie agreed to break off all ties with
his former SS associates. This Barbie was willing to do.

A new network of informants was established and given
the code name "Petersen." Barbie and Merk became the
leaders of the Petersen Network, which consisted of 52
informants throughout Europe.

Agent Taylor worked from a "safe house" in Memmingen. He was very impressed with Barbie, claiming that he
was a strong anti-communist and Nazi idealist who felt
betrayed by the Nazis in power. Taylor ran the network
until the summer of '47. Although Taylor knew that
Regions I and III were looking for Barbie in Stuttgart and
Marburg, he did not inform headquarters for two months
that Barbie was part of the Petersen Network.

In the summer of 1947, Taylor was replaced by CIC agent
Camille Hajdu, who worked from a safe house in Kauf-

beuren. Hajdu, too, was impressed with the successful results achieved by Merk and Barbie. Ninety percent of the intelligence obtained by Hajdu's office was produced by the Petersen Network.

On December 11, 1947, Barbie was sent to the European Command Intelligence Center (ECIC) at Oberursel, near Frankfurt, for "detailed interrogation." The operations officer of CIC Headquarters sent interrogation instructions to ECIC requesting that Barbie be interrogated only about his postwar activities.

CIC Headquarters was apparently not interested in Barbie's wartime experiences. Region IV and Agent Hajdu were not at all pleased with Barbie's arrest. They requested some type of preferential treatment. Lt. Col. Ellington Golden, who had replaced Lt. Col. Garvey, requested that Barbie be permitted to return to Region IV at the end of his interrogation.

It is totally incomprehensible to me that CIC requested ECIC not to go into Barbie's background. Because Region IV had an overriding interest in using Barbie as an informant, no one wanted to know what he had done during the war. Former Gestapo and SD agents were no longer considered a security threat. By the time Barbie was sent to ECIC, Allied authorities believed that remnants of the Nazi regime were no longer a danger to the Allied occupation.

Denazification was in full swing. Millions of Germans had filled out lengthy questionnaires *(Fragebogen)*, and the GI's were teaching the Germans to play baseball, although soccer *(Fussball)* remained their favorite sport. The objective was to obliterate all vestiges of Hitlerism and turn the Germans into freedom loving, democratically minded people.

HEADQUARTERS

COUNTER INTELLIGENCE CORPS REGION IV

970TH COUNTER INTELLIGENCE CORPS DETACHMENT

CSH/
APO 407-A
US ARMY

File No. IV-014

SECRET

21 November 1947

MEMORANDUM FOR THE OFFICER IN CHARGE

SUBJECT: BARBIE, Klaus, alias BECKER, BEHRENDS, MERTENS, SPEER and HOLZER.

    1. Reference operation SELECTION BOARD. Following information is herewith submitted regarding subject, as directed by S-3, Headquarters Region IV, CIC.

    2. a. Subject was originally contacted by Special Agent ROBERT S TAYLOR, on 18 May 1947 through informant X-3067-IV-K, who was running a network of informants for Special Agent Taylor. After an interview with Special Agent Taylor, subject was integrated into the network of X-3067*W-K*

    b. Subject, who has extensive connections with high level former German intelligence circles, immediately began exploiting these contacts and furnished this organization with extremely good material.

    c. In July 1947, subject was designated by X-3067-*IV-K* as his assistant and as such took over that portion of the net which specializes on French intelligence activities in the French and US zones of Germany. In this capacity subject has so far demonstrated exceedingly successful results.

    d. Since taking over Special Agent Taylor's net, this agent has had several conversations with subject and has scrutinized subject's work very carefully, and it is believed that subject has devoted all his efforts to his work.

    e. Although it is fully realized that as a member of operation SELECTION BOARD, subject's interrogation would reveal information of value, it is also felt that his arrest and possibly his delivery to British authorities would damage considerably the trust and faith which informants place in this organization.

REGRADED CONFIDENTIAL BY AUTHORITY OF
Det. 14 JULY 1950

- 1 -

-2-

Page 1 of 2 pages
Copy 1 of 6 copies
T-528

REGRADED UNCLASSIFIED
ON 21 JUL 1983
BY CDR USAINSCOM FOIPO

54

3. AGENT'S COMMENTS:

a. It is strongly recommended that subject not be arrested.

b. It is further recommended that, inasmuch as subject has in the past shown his willingness to answer any questions, subject's interrogation be conducted on a voluntary basis.

c. In accordance with above recommendations, it is requested that subject's interrogation be conducted by Headquarters Region IV, or that arrangements be made to avoid that subject be incarcerated or in any way treated as a prisoner while being interrogated.

d. It is believed that if above recommendations are taken into consideration, subject will voluntarily submit to any interrogation and that subject's services to this organization will not be lost. Furthermore the prestige which this organization enjoys with its informants will remain undamaged.

CAMILLE S. HAJDU
Special Agent, CIC

APPROVED:

PAUL O. GRUEHL
Special Agent, CIC
S-3

Page 2 of 2 pages
Copy 1 of 6 copies TS 28

7970 TH CIC GROUP
REGIONAL MAP

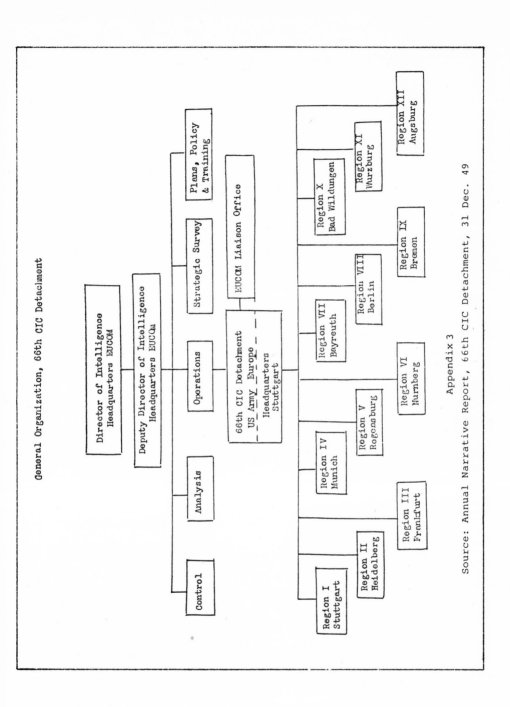

General Organization, 66th CIC Detachment

Appendix 3

Source: Annual Narrative Report, 66th CIC Detachment, 31 Dec. 49

57

CHAPTER I

ORGANIZATION

1. General Organization

The 6th CIC Detachment is the principal counter-intelligence investigative agency of the European Command and is under the operational jurisdiction of the Director of Intelligence, EUCOM. For operational purposes it is divided into a headquarters and twelve regions; the regions in turn maintain maximum coverage through eleven field offices, thirty resident offices and twenty-four day offices, in addition to the twelve regional headquarters. The preceding regional map shows the division of the US Zone of Germany into CIC regions and the location of their headquarters. Detachment Headquarters is located in Stuttgart and attached to Stuttgart Military Post for logistical support. Chart 1 illustrates the general organization of the Detachment.

-5-

CHAPTER II

OPERATIONS

1. **Mission**

    a. **Basic Mission.** The basic mission of the 66th CIC Detachment
is to protect the US Zone of Occupation in Germany against espionage,
sabotage and subversion, and to discharge such other investigative
duties as may be assigned by the Commander-in-Chief, EUCOM. The
Detachment is responsible for all counter intelligence operations of
a zone-wide nature. Other CIC units, not a part of this organization
and attached to the US Constabulary, 1st Division and US Air Forces
Europe, are responsible for the internal security of their own
installations and personnel. The 66th CIC Detachment is an informa-
tion-gathering agency as well as an investigative agency. The
primary function of its operating personnel is the collection, colla-
tion, evaluation, and classification of information of counter intelli-

-12-

gence interest for further analysis and dissemination by higher headquarters.

b. Specific Responsibilities. The following specific responsibilities have been charged to the Detachment in the fulfillment of its
basic mission:

(1) Discover, prevent, and counter the activities of foreign
intelligence services, secret police, and dissident or resistance groups.

(2) Protect US interests against sabotage and investigate
sabotage incidents.

(3) Detect, prevent, and neutralize subversion.

(4) Prevent the reorganization of ex-enemy intelligence services, security and secret police and para-military organizations.

(5) Support and assist the US occupational government agencies
as directed.

(6) Conduct investigations for immigration to the United States.

(7) Conduct security investigations when so directed.

(8) Perform interrogations and render reports with regard to
scientists in the US Zone.

(9) Conduct security surveys of US installations.

(10) Conduct background investigations.

(11) Furnish spot reports and coverage on any situation, incident or personality of potential security interest.

(12) Report positive intelligence information coming to CIC
attention in pursuit of its normal mission.

-13-

(13) Collect and evaluate positive military order of battle
intelligence outside the US occupied areas of Germany as directed.

2. Current Objectives

a. Screening. The screening of applicants for immigration to the
United States under the DP Act of 1948, a program which was begun in the
last quarter of 1948 and reached its peak in the second quarter of 1949,
continued to be the first priority mission of the Detachment. During
the period of this report, 5883 visa applications were screened, bringing
the total to 61,122 as of 31 December 1949.

b. Counter Subversion. Activities and personalities of left wing
political parties, with special emphasis on the Kommunistische Partei
Deutschland (KPD) and its counterpart in the Soviet Zone of Germany, the
Sozialistische Einheitspartei Deutschland (SED),were the major objectives
of the Counter Subversion Desk.

c. ~~Positive Intelligence~~. The attention of the Positive Intelligence Desk was centered on gathering order of battle information with
regard to Soviet ground forces stationed in the Soviet Zone of Germany.

d. Counter Espionage. The detection and neutralization of Czech
and Soviet espionage agents and nets in the US Zone were the primary
targets of the Counter Espionage Desk.

e. Security. Continuing primary objectives of the Security Desk
included hidden arms caches in the US Zone, renewal of interest and activity
with regard to gliding and glider pilots, and scientists in the US Zone,

-14-

listed by the Joint Intelligence Objective Agency (JIOA).

3. Current Operations

 a. Case Statistics. Although no large unit operations were completed during the period of this report, the following types and number of investigations were completed by the Detachment:

	For the period reported	For the year 1949
Total	10,216	63,644
Espionage	518	2812
Sabotage	6	93
Treason	2	14
Sedition	0	3
Subversive Activity	51	1070
Disaffection	6	19
Loyalty	76	414
Violation of AR 380-5	14	39
Security Surveys	5	460
Political Subversion		
Left Wing	702	4356
Right Wing	219	1313
Dissident Groups	74	409
Screenings		
Displaced Persons	7287	41,931

-15-

	For the period reported	For the year 1949
Exit from Germany	470	3039
Other	350	1431
Scientific	30	250
Positive Intelligence	334	2211
Border	23	166
Miscellaneous	249	3614
File checks	96,351	604,022

b. <u>Microfilming Project.</u> ~~████████████████████████~~ l
~~██~~
~~████████████~~ was begun by the Photo Lab in the first quarter of
1949. Although hampered by inadequate equipment, work on the project
continued during the period of this report. Meanwhile, the S-4 Section
was doing everything possible to obtain more and better equipment from
the ZI.

c. ~~██~~.
Early in September a project to inventory all Top Secret material contained in the dossiers of the Central Registry was undertaken. As a
result of this inventory, it was ~~████████████████████████████~~
~~██~~
~~██~~t
~~██~~t. This
project was of such magnitude that it required the assignment to Detach-

-16-

additional pages not declassified

63

Replacement personnel unqualified

Today many former agents attempt to rationalize our mistakes by contending that the U.S. personnel of the period lacked the necessary qualifications. Most of the replacements did not have war experience and were inclined to forgive former Nazis more readily than those who did. Many former Gestapo and SS leaders were found innocent of war crimes, released from internment camps, and hired as CIC informants. Furthermore, the old Nazis knew where such booty as German weapons, insignia, oil paintings, crystal, and china could be obtained. Because incoming staff had been unable to secure such souvenirs, they were not averse to using the former Nazis to lead them to these desirable items, which could be paid for with American cigarettes.

It was important for intelligence units in occupied Germany to produce the right information. We had to learn what was going on; we needed to see the big picture. Without the services of informants, we would have been in very bad shape.

Our system operated in much the same way that government authorities plea-bargain with known criminals—promising reduced sentences in return for cooperation and information. Plea-bargains, however, don't include being let off scot-free and paid to get out of the country!

Barbie as informant: asset or liability?

Since my February 1983 revelation that Barbie had been a paid informant, many former CIC agents who knew him have tried to somehow excuse his employment by CIC. The most common claims are that they didn't know the extent of his involvement in war crimes in France. They also claim that as a trained intelligence officer, Barbie could be valuable to the Americans. If a CIC agent assigned to a network of German informants was not fluent in the language—if the agent knew only "tourist" German *(Wo ist das Hotel?)*—the informant could easily turn the tables on the agent. The informant would assume the dominant role; the interrogator would become the person interrogated.

Barbie had, in fact, become a CIC agent and no one wanted to sever the relationship with him. If the French were to capture him, they would learn of previous CIC actions against the French as well as a great deal about CIC's overall operation. The operations officer in Augsburg in 1950 commented that Barbie "knows more about CIC targets, modus operandi, and essential elements of information, etc., than most CIC agents."

Colonel Earl Browning claimed that in 1947 Barbie lacked notoriety. It was known that as an SD, Barbie was a fugitive. To turn Barbie, Merk, and Merk's mistress over to the French in 1947 would have been a tremendous intelligence coup for CIC, and created notoriety worthy of several promotions. The political climate, however, promised even greater advantages if they were used as informants.

Former high Nazi officials were also used as informants because of tremendous competition among the various American intelligence units. We all wanted to beat the other units to a big story. Every arm of the military had its intelligence unit, and the rivalry was very keen. One organization had no idea what another was doing; we often arrested each other's informants. On several occasions we had to go to German jails to obtain the release of our low-priority informants. Everybody was spying on everybody else.

Former CIC office building in Augsburg.

4 Barbie Worked For Me

Starting anew in the old country

In August of 1946 I returned to the United States with my wife, Jenny, and our three month old daughter, Shirley. I was discharged from the army, as a major on November 6. After six months in the U.S., my wife was very homesick. Letters from her parents in Liège, Belgium, contributed to our decision to return to Europe, where several attempts to establish myself in an export/import business failed. Europe's postwar economic depression and difficulties in obtaining the work permit required for a foreigner living in Belgium were among the problems.

The occupation of Germany was in full swing. On February 3, 1948, I applied for a job as a U.S. civilian at the headquarters of the 970th CIC detachment in Frankfurt, Germany. When the administrative officer interviewed me and learned that I could speak German and French fluently, he hired me on the spot.

Former US Military Government and Military Police Headquarters
in Augsburg

I become a member of the CIC

I spent the next four weeks in Frankfurt familiarizing myself with the overall operation. In March, I was assigned to Region IV, which had its headquarters in Munich. The commanding officer was Lt. Col. Ellington Golden. After only a few days in Munich, the colonel assigned me to his sub-region in Augsburg, 25 miles northwest on the *Autobahn* from Munich.

I was well qualified by my wartime experience as a POW interrogator and my training at the Military Intelligence School at Camp Ritchie, Maryland, to handle German informants. When I arrived in Augsburg, I was told by the administrator of the sub-region, Capt. George M. Spiller, that I had been sent to him to handle a special assignment.

I spent the next two weeks settling into my new quarters. I was assigned to a lovely single-family house requisitioned by the army on Warndtstrasse 26. My next step was to move my wife and daughter from Liège to Augsburg.

It didn't take me long to learn the ins and outs of the CIC sub-region. Most of the personnel served administrative functions. Of the 15-member staff who made up the complement of the sub-region, I was the only one who spoke German.

During the next several weeks I interrogated a number of suspicious characters picked up by our Military Police. We were particularly interested in all border crossers who had recently been in the Soviet Zone of Occupation. Most of my subjects were turned over to the American Criminal Investigation Division (CID) in Augsburg because they were involved in some form of black market activity or lacked adequate identification papers.

Barbie assignment begins

Suddenly, at the end of May, Capt. Spiller called me into his office and said very secretively, "Dabby, the assignment for which you were hired is about to begin. I have specific instructions from Munich that you are to take over the direction of a special network of German informants. They have been on the CIC payroll for over a year and have produced some of our outfit's most successful espionage work. I personally do not know what it's all about, but I have orders to send you to the town of Memmingen, where you will report to another CIC sub-region for further instructions. Tell our motor pool sergeant, Sammy Denato, to get a three-quarter ton truck ready for you so that you can pick up some special people and their luggage. Bring them to Augsburg, where we have a house ready for them on Mozartstrasse 10."

According to the Ryan Report, my takeover of the net occurred on June 15, 1948. According to my own calculations, it had to have taken place at least a month earlier—when I met Barbie, he informed me that he had just returned from the European Command Interrogation Center (ECIC) in Oberursel, from which the Ryan Report says he was released on May 10, 1948.

Upon my arrival in Memmingen, I was met by an American in civilian clothes who would not introduce himself. He did tell me, however, that I was not yet at my proper destination. He then produced a slip of paper with the names Kurt Merk and Klaus Barbie, and the address Schillerstrasse 7, in Kempten, written on it. Without further instructions or a briefing of any kind, he said, "Drive to Kempten and pick up the people who are waiting for you. Take them to Augsburg, where you will be working with them."

I easily found the address on Schillerstrasse. When I rang the doorbell, a stocky, round-faced man opened the door. When I asked if Klaus Barbie lived here, he immediately replied, "Come on in. I am Klaus Barbie. You must be Mr. Dabringhaus. I've been waiting for you."

It quickly became apparent that Barbie, the German informant, knew more about our CIC operation than I did. At Region IV Headquarters, technical specialist Lt. Richard K. Lavoie, who was in charge of the overall direction of the network, had not seen fit to brief me on these special German informants. He dropped me cold turkey into their laps. I never did meet Lavoie face-to-face but I did have some correspondence with him. In addition to Col. Golden, the only others I remember were our operations officer, whose name was Capt. Rausch, and Capt. Etkin, who later replaced him.

The whole situation seemed to me to be very unprofessional. I was given the impression that I was there as a mere errand boy for Barbie and his friends. I sat down in the front room and continued to talk to Barbie. He claimed he was glad to move to Augsburg, a much larger city than Kempten, where he had grown uneasy and bored. He seemed anxious to get to work, having been locked up at ECIC for five months, and genuinely happy to have a new handler. He was apparently calling all the shots. Since I had absolutely no idea who the other people in the house were, I decided to ask Barbie a few questions. He did not hesitate to tell me that he had been a captain in the SD, stationed in Lyons, France, from 1942/44. He boasted that he was one of Germany's most successful intelligence agents and that he had penetrated the *maquis*, one of the names by which the underground was known. "I've been doing the same work for the Americans for over a year," he said. "With your help we'll do even better."

As a member of SD, Barbie had been directly responsible to Himmler's Security Headquarters, (RSHA), which in the last years of the war was the real center of Nazi power. He should have been arrested immediately after the war by the occupation forces, since all SD members were listed on the Automatic Arrest Category.

After the German victory over France in May 1940, the German army observed strict military protocol. A large

*Schillerstrasse 7, Kempten. The house where Barbie and Merk lived
before I moved them to Augsburg.*

number of collaborators flocked to assist the Germans. Even a considerable number of the French intelligentsia were misled. The German propaganda machine had been so successful and the behavior of the German army generally so "correct" in Prussian military terms that the French countryside was nearly paralyzed from 1940 to 1942. Rumor had it that in 1940 the first German reconnaisance troops had actually paid for their gas at the gas stations. This idyllic notion came to an abrupt end in 1942 when the SS sent its henchmen into France. The execution of hostages and the torture of resistance fighters permanently altered the image of the German army in France.

I meet Merk and his mistress

But I had not come to arrest Barbie. I had come to work with him, and I assumed that the people at CIC headquarters knew what they were doing. At that moment another man entered the room. He had approximately the same build as Barbie but his hair was a darker brown. Barbie introduced him to me as Kurt Merk, a captain in the German counterintelligence *(Abwehr)*. Because Merk was not SS like Barbie, I felt slightly relieved, although, as an intelligence officer, he, too, should have been arrested for detailed interrogation about his work. I liked Merk better than Barbie right from the beginning. He explained to me that he and Barbie knew each other from having worked together in France. Merk left the room briefly, returning with an attractive young lady whom he introduced as Andree Simone Rivez, his future bride. He said that they had met in France.

I was surprised to find her there but could readily see that Merk was not about to leave his future wife behind. Andree was tall, nearly a head taller than Merk, attractive and statuesque. What was a Frenchwoman doing in bombed-out Germany? Merk explained that she had been a valuable informant for him during the occupation of France. He

*Mozartstrasse 10, Stadtbergen on the outskirts of Augsburg. Barbie's
and Merk's residence in Augsburg.*

certainly could not leave her in France, where she would have been tried for treason and, in all probability, executed.

Dr. Augsburg and his "final solutions"

I was about ready to say that we should pack up and leave for Augsburg when another man entered the room. He was introduced to me as Professor Emil Augsburg, another member of the Merk-Barbie network of informants. Professor Augsburg, a former colonel in the SS, had at one time been a member of the infamous Wannsee Institute. This institute was instrumental in developing the so-called "final solution" to the "Jewish problem". Dr. Augsburg was later assigned to the East Institute, whose mission was to prepare a similar "final solution" for the Russian population.

According to Dr. Augsburg, the East Institute convened in the city of Königsberg, from 1941 to 1943, for the purpose of devising a satisfactory means of eliminating the Russian population after the German victory. The institute members, who were appointed by Heinrich Himmler, were mainly high-ranking SS officers. As I listened to Dr. Augsburg's account of the past, I recalled that Hitler's goals included not only the extermination of the Jews but also the total annihilation of all of his enemies.

Many members of special SS formations were tried as war criminals between 1946 and 1948 for their efforts to carry out orders devised by Hitler's East Institute which included the subjugation and extermination of those who lived in the conquered eastern regions. German troops rounded up civilians, destroyed their villages, and retained them as hostages. As an arbitrary reprisal measure, hostages were executed at a ratio of one hundred to one for the death of each German soldier. Even the regular army was committed to rounding up Jews, Gypsies, and other "undesirable" persons to be turned over to the SS for liquidation. The East Institute's resettlement program had a dual purpose: to destroy the culture and the very existence of the conquered peoples of the east and to settle German nationals in their place. These were only a few of the options proposed by the institute, which was chaired by Alfred Rosenberg, Hitler's so-called racial expert.

Why was I not warned about the caliber of the people I was to deal with? Did my lack of knowledge serve a definite purpose or was it a tremendous oversight? The informants may have wanted to test my initial reactions to decide whether I would be a suitable control officer for the network. My first thought was get the hell out of that house, but I quickly remembered my role as an intelligence officer and regained my composure.

I explained to Barbie, "Since Dr. Augsburg really has no experience in intelligence work, I suggest that he remain here in Kempten."

I saw no necessity for him to join us in Augsburg, since the slip of paper I had received in Memmingen had only named Merk and Barbie. The doctor was actually carried on the roster of the Merk-Barbie Network as a sub-source. It appeared to me that he could work from his present address in Kempten, so I decided to leave him behind. "We better get started," I told them. "It is about a one hour ride, and you will need some time to get settled into your new house."

Barbie rode up in the cab with me and Merk and his mistress climbed in the back after we had stored six or seven suitcases and several heavy boxes on the floor of the truck.

Base established in Augsburg

We arrived in Augsburg, at the house on Mozartstrasse 10, around 5 o'clock in the evening. It was a large, single-family house, but designed so that two families could comfortably occupy it. Merk and his mistress took one side of the house, and Barbie moved into the other side. I was curious as to why

The Barbie-Merk safehouse at Mozartstrasse 10, Stadtbergen on the outskirts of Augsburg. Merk and his mistress lived on one side of the house, while Barbie lived on the other side. Barbie's family would also live there when they visited him.

Municipal swimming pool Augsburg where I worked with Merk and Barbie in 2nd floor offices.

we had picked out such a large house for three people, but soon learned that the mother of Merk's mistress would be a frequent visitor. Barbie's wife and two children, who lived in the city of Trier, would also visit for long periods of time. Several weeks later I discovered that even though I had left Dr. Augsburg in Kempten, he and his secretary spent much time in the Augsburg house.

It must be made clear that none of these well-paid informants were under American military surveillance. They were as free as any German living in the Occupied Zone of Germany. They could come and go as they pleased. A few days after our arrival in Augsburg, Barbie visited his family in Trier for a long weekend. In addition to a generous assortment of benefits—such as free housing, supplies, and money, which added up to about $2,000 a month overall—they also enjoyed the protection of the American army. For a bunch of war criminals on the wanted list, this was a pretty nice arrangement.

I suggested to Merk that our operation would have a more professional appearance if we operated from an office instead of my coming to their house. We found three large offices that would serve our purposes in a large building that contained the municipal swimming pool. The offices had several exits and one entrance with a long staircase leading from the sidewalk up to the second floor. They were immediately adjacent to the main entrance of the municipal swimming pool, which enabled us to come and go without arousing suspicion.

Three days after we set up shop in these offices, Merk and Barbie surprised me by hiring a secretary. She was an attractive, blond woman who explained to me that she was a widow, having lost her SS husband on the Eastern Front. "I have occasionally worked for Dr. Augsburg and Kurt Merk, and I have just moved up from Kempten."

She was an efficient secretary, who typed all of the reports that Merk and Barbie gave her. This made it easy for me to translate them into English before submitting them by messenger to Lavoie, the technical specialist at Region IV in Munich.

Individual missions selected

We decided that Merk would be used to penetrate illegal Soviet organizations in the American Zone and generally keep tabs on all French activities. Four of the network's sub-sources lived in the French Zone of Occupation and had good connections with French intelligence. Barbie was given the mission of penetrating the communist party in Bavaria.

Both objectives were met, with remarkable results. In August of 1948 I was informed by Lavoie that the Petersen Network had proved to be one of the most fruitful sources of information for Region IV. It was an exceptionally skillful intelligence net, whose missions and targets could be changed at a moment's notice.

We become temporary communists

One of Barbie's former SS connections had been a concentration camp guard. One day, on a street in Augsburg, he saw a former communist who had been an inmate in the camp for ten years. The inmate had survived by functioning as a stool pigeon for the SS.

Barbie and I arranged to meet this former communist to try to turn him around one more time and get him to work for the Americans. We had recently received instructions from headquarters to make every effort to penetrate the communist party in Bavaria. We had learned that communists were instigating labor strikes throughout the occupied zone, and this Augsburg communist could help us verify these allegations.

I interrogated the man without Barbie's presence. He did not hesitate to tell me his entire story. He was a committed communist during the Weimar Republic (1918 to 1933), having fought with deep personal conviction against both proponents of German nationalism and Social Democrats. To prove his point, he mentioned that in 1931 a special communist committee assigned him to blow up the city hall in the Bavarian town of Füssen. He didn't remember why they picked on the city hall, but he accepted the assignment without question. "I obtained dynamite and packed a knapsack with explosives. The party gave me just enough money for the train fare from Augsburg to Füssen and back. I set the explosives during the night near the front entrance. The explosion made a sizable hole in the main part of the entrance hall, but since the building was not occupied at the time, I didn't hurt anybody."

"Soon after Hitler seized power in 1933," he continued, "I was among the first communists sent to the concentration camp at Dachau. After several years of mistreatment, abuse, and torture, I was approached by one of the SS guards to become a camp stool pigeon. The guard made it perfectly clear that if I refused, the lives of my wife and children would be in danger. I'm not proud of what I did, but I'm convinced that because of my collaboration, my whole family is alive today."

I listened to the man's story attentively and then said, "I can certainly understand your motives and I am glad that your wife and children survived. However, if you were willing to help the Nazis, it shouldn't be so difficult for you to help the Americans now. All you have to do is to take my friend Barbie and me to your next communist meeting in Augsburg and introduce us to your friends as good communists from out of town. I can assure you that no one will ever learn that you were at one time a stoolie for the SS." He realized that he was in a bind and unhesitatingly agreed to our plan.

Barbie and I attended the next meeting of the communist party in Augsburg along with our new informant. To make me look more like a real German, Barbie had suggested that I have a suit made by a German tailor, which I did. It was made of the same poor quality cloth, laced with cellulose, like most German suits were at that time.

At the Augsburg city clerk's office I had an identification card made; I used the name Richard Holthof. My ID card showed that I was born in Essen, which I could under no circumstances deny because of the way I spoke German. The moment I opened my mouth to speak, my accent would place me in the Rhenish-Westphalian region. For my occupation I had written down laboratory assistant. The clerk stamped in big block letters across the front of the ID card that I had been "denazified."

Barbie went with me to the town hall because he also needed a new ID card. He had used the aliases Becker, Mertens, and Spehr. Now he wanted an ID card bearing the name Klaus Holzer. He examined my ID card to make sure it was properly filled out, and that the photo and stamps were in the right places. He then asked me to remind the clerk not to forget the denazification stamp on his new card. He complained that on his previous ID card they forgot to put the big red stamp across the front of the cover. He almost got arrested in Munich when a policeman pointed out to him that the stamp was mandatory. The absence of the stamp implied that he had not properly passed the denazification court *(Spruchkammer)*.

On July 20, 1948, I accompanied Barbie to my first communist party meeting. The meeting was held in the back room of a beer garden on the edge of Augsburg. Our new communist informant introduced Barbie and me to the chairman of the meeting. We were given a pleasant welcome and took our seats in the middle of a long table.

After 17 people had been seated around the table, the chairman opened the meeting. Barbie and I were introduced as comrades from out of town, Barbie from Trier and I from Essen. We were welcomed with applause, and a few *prosts*, with beer glasses raised high.

Our new communist sub-source received congratulations for bringing two new members and the chairman urged everyone present to campaign enthusiastically for new comrades. I was very nervous at the beginning of the meeting and nearly blew my cover. I put out a cigarette in an ashtray in front of me and left the butt there instead of putting it in my pocket, like everyone else was doing. There were plenty of ashtrays on the table, but although many of the members were smoking, there wasn't a single cigarette butt in the ashtrays. I'd forgotten that Germany was still on a cigarette-butt economy. Barbie quickly poked me in the ribs and glanced at the ashtray where my cigarette butt was still faintly smoldering. Realizing my mistake, I reached for the cigarette and rubbed the burning end until the fire was totally extinguished. I then carefully put the butt back in my coat pocket.

During the official meeting, discussion centered around the instigation of strikes in major industries. Reference was made to a strike then in progress at the Augsburg gas works. One member, an employee of the gas works, made suggestions on how to expand the strike. He reported that he had only been able to persuade two or three stokers to stay away from the job. If he could convince the rest of the stokers to stay home, the gas works would have to shut down.

After an hour and a half the meeting was adjourned without much fanfare. Barbie and I both promised to return for the next meeting if we were still in town. From that day on our new communist informant kept us abreast of all activities and future plans of the communist cell in Augsburg.

Politics and potatoes

The next day I decided to do some investigating. At the
Augsburg gas works, the situation was a far cry from what
had been depicted at the party meeting the night before. I
learned that with the exception of one or two workers, none
were communists or even had radical leanings. A few stokers
had not turned up for work, but only because they were sick.
Three of them had fainted the day before from the heat and
from improper nourishment. Men performing heavy labor
were supposed to receive extra rations.

Communists were exploiting the scarcity of food in
Germany. A whole freight car full of American lard, destined
for Augsburg, had been standing on a railroad siding in
northern Germany for two weeks. By investigating all of the
local transport companies, I located the bill of lading
assigning this particular shipment to Augsburg. Upon my
request, the owner of the company put a tracer on the
shipment, and a few days later the lard arrived in the
distribution centers. The delay was most likely instigated by
communist workers on the railroad.

The German people experienced food shortages after both
World War I and World War II. But the Germans will not
starve as long as they have potatoes. No people on earth utilize
the potato in as many different ways as the Germans. The
next most important ingredient is some form of shortening,
preferably lard. With potatoes and lard, a German can
survive. After the workers at the gas works received their
additional rations, the communist-instigated strike was a
fizzle. All the workers returned to their jobs, and the
communist party in Augsburg discussed other means of
causing unrest in local industries.

Through the help of Barbie's SS sub-source and his
communist stool pigeon, we knew just about everything that
the fledgling communist party in Bavaria was doing.
Barbie's value was further enhanced when he received the

credit for this infiltration. The reputation of the Petersen Network grew by leaps and bounds.

Merk and Barbie accepted any new mission I was asked to assign them. These missions often included sending sub-sources to contact friends in the Soviet Zone, Czecho-slovakia, and Romania. The information that Merk and Barbie produced and I translated to send to our head-quarters was recognized by my superiors as the most important intelligence received by CIC.

The high cost of spying

During this time both Merk and Barbie complained that they weren't receiving enough money. "In order to operate the network as efficiently as you demand, we need the equivalent of $2,000 to $2,500 per month," Merk argued.

Barbie said that instead of D-marks, ration cards, and cigarettes, he would prefer to have American dollars. He pointed out that several of his informants were living outside of Germany, where only green dollars could be exchanged for local currency. He insisted that he lost much valuable time and occasionally had to use personal couriers to sell his cigarettes and supplies on the black market in Munich in order to obtain American dollars. He could not understand why CIC couldn't pay the network directly in American currency. I passed their concerns on to technical specialist Lavoie. Lavoie and the operations officer handled payments to the network and kept records of the amounts of money allocated to Merk, Barbie, and their informants.

After each payday Merk and Barbie argued about the division of funds. One day Barbie turned to me and said, "Dabringhaus, you've got to impress upon your supervisors that I need more money, especially real dollars, to operate efficiently. I really do believe I'm worth more money than I'm getting. I can barely take care of my sub-sources."

"I will pass your request up to higher headquarters," I replied, "but I suggest you talk to Lt. Lavoie yourself the next time you are in Munich."

However, when I once asked Barbie why I hadn't received any good information for over a week, he answered that he was waiting for reports from informants in the field. A few days later I overheard him dictating a report to our secretary, reading from a German newspaper. The article was credited to a Yugoslavian news agency. I told Barbie, "You do not have to pad your reports with newspaper articles. I can read them myself." His reply was that I was putting too much pressure on him for information.

Merk reveals Barbie's monstrous crimes

Money played an important role in Barbie's life, and serious arguments developed between Merk and Barbie concerning the division of their funds. When Barbie was sent to ECIC for two weeks of further interrogation in July 1948, Merk took me aside and confided, "You should know that Barbie's work is not worth the money he is receiving. All the fancy reports that we have submitted recently were produced by me and my informants. All he has done this summer is dig up the informant to penetrate the communist party in Augsburg. You and I have done the real work."

I hardly knew how to answer, but since I had liked Merk better than Barbie from the beginning, I said, "I believe you, Kurt, but what makes you bring up money at this time?"

Very calmly Merk continued, "Barbie would work for nothing if you Americans ever found out what he did in France while he was in charge of an SD special commando in Lyons."

I pressed Merk for details. He seemed hesitant to continue the conversation, so I prodded him by saying, "I suspect that

Barbie was a brutal interrogator. The SD was known to use force and beat prisoners who wouldn't talk."

"That doesn't even scratch the surface!" Merk continued. "He is high on the wanted list in France for murder. If the French ever find the mass graves for which Barbie is responsible, you will be forced to turn him over to them."

In disbelief and shock I asked, "How do you know all this if you worked in Dijon and Barbie in Lyons?"

"You can believe me!" Merk emphasized. "In 1943 and '44 I had occasion to work directly with Barbie in Lyons on several espionage cases and I saw with my own eyes some 200 resistance fighters that Barbie had ordered strung up by their thumbs in the Gestapo Headquarters in Fort Montluc. In spite of being tortured, they had all refused to collaborate. Barbie gave orders for them to hang there until they were dead."

"Kurt, are you making this up?" I asked. "What a story! If this can be verified, I'm working with a first-class war criminal, and he should be turned over to the French."

"Of course I am sure," he said. "During our stay in France I sometimes worked with Barbie personally. I'm very familiar with the brutality he employed. Some of the soldiers in Barbie's SD command told me about the animalistic behavior for which Barbie's unit received several commendations. Please be careful to whom you tell this story. Barbie has strong supporters in your CIC headquarters. Should he ever be confronted with information about these atrocities, he will know immediately that I have talked to you."

I began to realize why I had disliked Barbie from the beginning. A strong feeling of abhorrence came over me as my suspicions were confirmed. Barbie had told me earlier that he and Merk had worked on some high-level intelligence operations in France. Barbie knew all about the role of Merk's mistress, Andree Rivez, in helping him break up three large resistance groups in Dijon and Lyons.

Young prisoner forced to act as bait

To underscore their value to CIC and to obtain larger payments for their network, Merk and Barbie had spread the word that they were known as Germany's best intelligence operatives in occupied France. With a great show of egotism, Barbie regaled me with the story of a spy thriller that he and Merk had been involved in.

The Germans knew that a British diplomatic courier frequently came to Vichy, France. Merk and Barbie decided that if they could photograph the contents of this courier's attaché case, they would both receive medals. As Barbie explained their scheme, "We provided him with a good-looking blonde informant during his stay in Vichy. When he didn't take the bait, we decided to send a redhead. She, too, struck out. On our third attempt, using a very attractive brunette, we again had no luck, even though the diplomat had invited her to have dinner with him."

Barbie and Merk came to the conclusion that the man was homosexual. In order to succeed in their mission, they searched for a handsome young man. Among Barbie's prisoners was a Jewish family about to be deported to a concentration camp in Germany. They had an 18-year-old son, who was chosen and briefed about the intended mission. "If you help us," Barbie said, "and succeed with this assignment, I promise that you and your family will be stricken from the list of prisoners going to Germany and you will be allowed to live free in southern France with my protection."

The boy reluctantly accepted the offer in order to save his family. With a smile of great self-importance, Barbie announced, "The young man returned after successfully accomplishing his mission."

Although Barbie insisted that he kept his promise regarding the Jewish family, I doubt that he did so. There was never any verification. I suspect that both Merk and

Barbie told the story to many CIC agents to prove what well-trained and exceptional operatives they were and that they were worth every penny that CIC was paying them.

I relay disclosures to headquarters

Merk's revelations were very exciting, to say the least. I immediately sent his juicy stories to my headquarters in Munich. I expected the CIC to come to arrest Barbie immediately and turn him over to the French. After hearing nothing for several weeks, I called Lt. Lavoie in Munich and asked him what decision had been reached regarding Barbie's war crimes. The operations officer in Munich, who picked up the phone, told me that my reports were terrific, but that no decision had been made. "Since you and Barbie are doing such a great job of penetrating the Augsburg communist party, we feel you should continue working with him. When the time is ripe, we will turn him over to the French." Being part of a military organization I had to work within channels; during those turbulant times I had no access to the press, and it was impossible to skip channels and go to higher headquarters directly. Where were the investigative reporters then?

Instead of being arrested, Barbie received an additional payment; and on September 5, 1948, I received a promotion from CAF-8 to CAF-9. It was obvious that this promotion was not for discovering Barbie's atrocities in France, but for penetrating the communist party in Augsburg.

Ryan Report pleads ignorance

The Ryan Report repeatedly states that CIC officials knew nothing about Barbie's background until May 14, 1949. Ryan writes, "On May 14, 1949—the date CIC officials were later to maintain was their first inkling that Barbie may have been a war criminal—a news item appeared in a Paris newspaper headlined: "Arrest Barbie our torturer!"

Either technical specialist Lavoie did not pass my reports on to higher headquarters, or no one in authority believed them. According to the Ryan Report, Joseph Vidal, technical specialist at CIC Headquarters, and Capt. Eugene Kolb stated that as of July, 1949, the French had given no indication that Barbie was involved in war crimes. All requests up to that time from the French Sureté had been centered on Barbie as a material witness in the Hardy case.

If my reports had gone to higher headquarters, CIC would certainly have known a year sooner—by the end of August, 1948—that they were dealing with a known war criminal. My reports are probably among those that, according to the Ryan Report, "could not be located and may have been destroyed long ago, perhaps shortly after they were submitted and analyzed." The report continues to state that transcripts of various interrogation reports could not be located in either U.S. or French archives.

It appears that the political climate in Europe continued to dictate the use of Barbie as an informant, and decisions were made by individual officers without consulting their superiors.

Barbie departure anticipated

My regional commander, Lt. Col. Ellington Golden, assured me that Barbie would be turned over to the French when his value as an informant was exhausted. With that in mind I reluctantly continued to work with the Petersen Network. I requested transfer to another assignment. I also applied for extended active duty in the army. Since the Berlin airlift was by then in full swing and talk of war with the Russians was widespread, I had reason to believe my application would be approved.

I continued my assignment, but my heart wasn't in it. To come to the office every morning knowing that I was working with a master war criminal dampened my spirits considerably. Barbie also seemed to have a change of attitude toward me personally. I became increasingly aware of the fact that Merk and Barbie rarely occupied our offices at the same time. I'm convinced that Barbie learned about Merk's revelations to me and that as a result their friendship began to deteriorate.

The Butcher's worries increase

Through Barbie's contact inside French intelligence headquarters in Baden Baden, Germany, he must have learned that the French were again looking for him. There is no doubt that Barbie knew that French agents were on the prowl before this information reached CIC Headquarters. He already knew that he was wanted as a witness in the Hardy trial in France. After I told him that on two separate occasions French agents had inquired as to his whereabouts, he became quite nervous and suspicious, and very security-minded. Whenever I came to the office a few minutes late and Barbie and the secretary were already there, he would look at the open door as though he expected someone to follow me in. He became more relaxed once the door was closed. One day I asked him, "Why are you so fidgety lately, Klaus?"

He replied, "I've got to think about my safety and that of my family. I know that the French have a dragnet out for me; if they ever get me to France, I'll never come back."

I assured him that as long as he was producing good information, he could count on the protection of CIC and the American Army.

I had recently had to lie to several French agents regarding the whereabouts of Klaus Barbie. If they had been more insistent and specific about Barbie's war crimes, I would probably have turned him over to the French. The deception that I was ordered to carry out made me uneasy. After all, the U.S. and France were Western Allies; we had fought together during the war and I have always admired the French people. I eventually attributed it all to the game of espionage. I wasn't even allowed to tell my wife what I was doing.

Thinking back to D-Day

My thoughts returned to D-Day, June 6, 1944, when I landed in Normandy with the First U.S. Infantry Division. The French had been demoralized by Germany's quick victory in 1940 and their four years of oppression during the German occupation. A proud and independent people had lost their self-esteem. When the Americans landed, we were not welcomed with open arms. Even after we had been there for several days, the French people were not yet ready to believe that the Americans, British, Canadians, and Poles had come to liberate them. They had been mesmerized by the propaganda that portrayed the German Army as invincible. On D-Day plus five I saw a French farm woman carrying a basket full of eggs from her hen house. We hadn't seen a fresh egg for weeks, so I dared to ask her for two of her eggs. The poor confused woman answered, "I've got to save these eggs for the Germans. They will be back tomorrow or the next day, and you will be swimming back to England."

One of my sergeants, who spoke better French than I did, finally persuaded her to part with a few eggs. The French people were so morally devastated that they found it difficult to accept liberation. We were thought of more as intruders than liberators.

In the town of La Ferte-Mace, which we reached after fighting a vicious battle in Domfront, I heard an elderly

Frenchman say, "It is regrettable that the Germans are leaving. They brought cleanliness and law and order to our town."

Such remarks did not sit well with the Americans, especially since we had just suffered heavy casualties during a fierce counterattack by the SS.

The vaunted French underground had not yet surfaced. The French Resistance Army did not turn up in full force until Paris was liberated in August of 1944. The French people had begun to breathe deeply once again and slowly came to realize that the nightmare of German occupation was over. The French liberation army, wearing the Cross of Lorraine on their armbands, began to assist in guarding German prisoners.

Fraternizing suspects have their heads shaved

One postwar practice of the French underground that shocked American soldiers was the rounding up for questioning of all women who had fraternized with Germans. Any girl who had slept with a German had her hair cut off and her head shaved. The women were loaded on open trucks and paraded through the towns, where they were pelted with stones and eggs, beaten with sticks, and frequently spat upon. Unfortunately, there were many false denunciations. If a girl had been seen even talking to a German soldier, she could be subjected to the same treatment. The American GI's were repelled by what they viewed as unfair treatment. Girls who feared these reprisals often offered themselves to our soldiers for protection. Many Americans found the system of punishment so distasteful that they fought with the French resistance fighters to prevent them from carrying out this form of retribution.

While talking to Merk and his mistress one day about my experience in France, I said to Andree, "It's a good thing Kurt brought you to Germany or you might have lost your beautiful auburn hair."

She promptly replied, "I would have lost more than my hair after what I did for this guy. I would have been guillotined!"

French Resistance fights on

France's resistance fighters fought hard and valuable battles, both behind and in front of our lines, and saved many American lives. Despite grim and bloody reprisals by the Germans against helpless civilians, resistance fighters continued their heroic efforts, achieving more than we Americans believed possible. I probably owe my life to a French worker in a munitions factory because an artillery shell, which landed within three yards of my position in Normandy, did not explode. It had been turned into a dud through crafty sabotage by French workers.

The famous Resistance-Fer, of which Col. Hardy was a leader, began to derail hundreds of German trains on the first day after D-Day. When the "Green Plan" *(Plan Vert)* for sabotaging rail lines in support of the allied landings went into effect, some 500 railway lines were cut. On June 7, the Resistance in Burgundy, the famous wine country of France, blew up so many railroad lines that traffic was stopped in all directions for many days. The Second SS Armored Division *Das Reich*, which was coming up from the south of France to reinforce the German troops against the Normandy beachhead, was delayed for nearly a week by resistance fighters who continued to attack the trains despite sustaining heavy losses. Information about the train movement was also radioed to London so that our air force would have an important target that day. I remember interrogating prisoners from that SS division and hearing them describe the horrors they encountered on their six-day train ride.

The Spiller story

In trying to get a new assignment after I learned of Barbie's war crimes, I approached my immediate superior, Capt. George M. Spiller, administrator of the sub-region. I told him what I had learned about Barbie from Kurt Merk and asked him to get me another assignment.

Spiller and I had never been very friendly, and he immediately turned me down. The Report of Efficiency Rating, which was signed by him on September 21, 1948, gave me only an official rating of "Good." How I had managed to get a promotion on September 5 with only an average rating from Capt. Spiller remains a mystery to me.

Spiller never liked anyone who spoke a foreign language. When he learned that I had married a girl from Liége, Belgium, he told me, "How in the hell can you marry a foreigner?"

We had very little social contact, and I was invited only once, with my wife, to a cocktail party at his house. He knew I outranked him in the military, and his resentment was obvious.

Spiller had little interest in the operation of his sub-region. He spent most of his weekends elsewhere. He had become an avid hunter, and one weekend he invited me to go along on a stag hunt in Oberstdorf. He was very familiar with the game warden *(Jägermeister)*, and even more so with his daughter. The game warden placed me in a runway, where he thought I would be able to get a shot at a nice buck. Unfortunately, none of us were successful that weekend.

It was common knowledge among CIC members of the sub-region that Spiller was diverting large quantities of supplies, including cases of cigarettes, to his girlfriend's house in Oberstdorf. It was relatively easy to attribute these vanishing supplies to the various members of the sub-region since we all used several cartons of cigarettes each week to pay our low-priority informants. It would have been difficult to determine whether any of the missing supplies had been destined for the Petersen Network, since Merk and Barbie picked up their payments of supplies directly from technical specialist Lavoie in Munich.

Spiller was a quiet man. One could even call him a loner. He occasionally checked up on Capt. George Friedman, who was screening displaced persons in a nearby Romanian camp, but spent most of his day in the main office looking after the routine operation of the sub-region. He showed absolutely no interest in my work with Barbie and Merk, although we were producing the hottest information in all of Region IV.

Six months after I left Augsburg, I heard through the grapevine that Spiller's misuse of supplies had been discovered. Cases of fine china and crystal, and oriental rugs were being shipped from his girlfriend's house to his home in the United States. He was reprimanded and reassigned to the United States.

After February 5, 1983, when I made Barbie's CIC connection public, I made every effort to locate my former sub-region commander Capt. Spiller. John Tipton, who was working for the intelligence committee of the House of Representatives, called me on February 21. Tipton had just talked to Mrs. Spiller in Dallas, Texas. Spiller, who had retired from the army after 30 years, had been selling automobiles in a Dallas showroom. On February 10, five days after my story broke, Spiller died of a massive heart attack. Mrs. Spiller, still in shock from losing her husband, confirmed to Tipton that they were indeed in Augsburg in 1948, and she remembered my name since it is an unusual, long German name.

It really grieves me to have to bring this out, but the record would not be complete without these observations on Spiller's background.

Spiller was a perfect example of an officer misplaced in his assignment. He had had no intelligence training. He never learned a word of German although he spent years of service in occupied Germany. I don't believe he could even say *"Gesundheit."* He had a total disregard for other cultures and considered all Germans living in Germany foreigners. He possessed no aptitude for intelligence work. He was the kind of American who tended to create the false impression that all Americans are cowboys.

CIC duties varied widely

The other 15 agents in our sub-region did their jobs conscientiously. Much of the work consisted of screening displaced persons. Large camps of Ukrainian and Romanian refugees were housed in former German barracks located in the Augsburg area. Another important part of our assignment was to interrogate black-market operators and persons without proper ID cards who had been turned over to us by the German police. After we had extracted any information that might be useful to CIC, we turned them over to the Criminal Investigation Department (CID) for further disposition.

Most of the other CIC agents in Augsburg were paper pushers. For that you didn't have to speak German. In the front office we employed a German receptionist who spoke both German and English. There was a big sign outside our office stating that we were CIC and anyone who wanted to talk to an American could come to our office. Some of our other assignments consisted of debriefing German prisoners recently returned from Russia, requisitioning houses for newly arrived American dependents, and establishing good relations with local German civil and police administrators.

There was an off-limits room in our office in Augsburg where all our classified documents were kept. An American female civilian employee, Spiller, and I were the only ones who had access to this room. The civilian employee was an excellent secretary. I dictated the translations of all Barbie's and Merk's reports to her. A daily courier from regional headquarters in Munich picked up our reports and dropped off supplies.

Secret Russian uranium mine uncovered

Although my personal enthusiasm for working with Barbie had diminished, our network continued to produce important information. During this period I was handed a report by Barbie that the Russians had placed a large section of the Soviet Zone near the Czech border off-limits. According to the report, the Russians were mining uranium ore in that region. This was a big scoop, and I impressed upon Barbie the importance of having his informant continue to bring as much information as possible. The United States thus far had a monopoly on the atomic bomb. An active uranium mining operation would certainly suggest that the Russians anticipated building an A-bomb themselves.

This kind of hot information certainly gave Barbie's value a boost in the eyes of my superiors. Nobody at headquarters would think seriously at that time about turning him over to the French for practical or political reasons. The network was involved in three main missions: 1) penetration of the Soviet Zone of Occupation, 2) penetration of French intelligence in Germany, and 3) infiltration of the communist party in Bavaria, which usually kept them very busy. Occasionally I would give Barbie a special assignment. I learned that a former high-ranking Nazi was still living illegally somewhere in Bavaria. Barbie, seemingly without a second thought, soon reported the name and address of the guy I was looking for and I had him picked up by the military police. At no time did Barbie ever hesitate to turn in his old buddies if he was asked to do so.

What made Barbie run?

What made this man change from a staunch Nazi SD operator into a proficient informant for American intelligence? Actually, by the time I met him, he was no longer simply an informant. He had so much information about the operation of CIC that he could be considered a real CIC agent. I, as the American control officer, really only functioned as a translator, messenger, and glorified errand boy. Neither Barbie nor Merk, turned from Nazi tool to American agent overnight.

After he left Lyons in late 1944, Barbie was chased through an assortment of allied camps, always managing to conceal his true identity. A serious wound on his left foot was bandaged for him in a French hospital. Whenever he felt that his interrogators were getting close to discovering his identity, he would escape from internment. It must be borne in mind that the French, British, and American prisoner of war enclosures were not carefully guarded.

Barbie once remarked that he had had a very tough time upon his return to Germany. He descended from SD captain and highly respected member of the SS to the status of a lowly beggar. "Until August 1945 I had to hide like a hunted animal," he recalled.

In the city of Kassel, in the American Zone, he was interned without his identity being discovered. He escaped from the Americans with a bicycle and went underground. A farmer gave him a place to stay, but he had to work very hard for his hiding place.

Six months later he left and tried his hand at black marketing. He had been in touch with other SS people who had taught him to forge ID cards. In November of 1946 he was arrested by British intelligence agents and sent to an internment camp in Hamburg. "After I had been there only a few days," he told me, "I walked right out of the camp past the sleeping guard."

British provide superb intelligence training

Later, when Barbie was working for CIC, he complained that the British had mistreated him during his imprisonment. My own experience makes this impossible to believe. As the captain of a prisoner of war interrogation team, I received the finest intelligence training from the British. The British had established a first-class interrogation center in the beautiful Cotswolds in England. A General Dispensary gave the center an excellent cover. German prisoners were brought there in ambulances. The American interrogators were permitted to observe the British interrogate and to practice interrogation on real prisoners. The British used clever tricks and ruses, but never force. Without this interrogation training in England, we Americans would have behaved like novices upon hitting the beaches in Normandy.

Bechtold takes over

When CIC learned that I had been called back to active duty, I was finally relieved of my assignment with Merk and Barbie. A sergeant by the name of Herbert Bechtold, who had been at Region IV Headquarters in Munich, was sent to Augsburg to take over. He had been briefed by Lavoie in Munich but I was given no opportunity to brief Bechtold in regard to my unique experience with the Petersen Network. Barbie was again allowed to look over his new agent to see whether they could work together. Apparently he passed the test. According to Bechtold's recent statements, he had no knowledge that Barbie was a war criminal. It is indeed strange that I, who among all of the agents had worked with the network the shortest period of time, was able to learn from Merk the extent of Barbie's atrocities in France.

Bechtold, Kolb deny knowledge of atrocities

Captain Eugene Kolb, and Bechtold, who have, since my exposure, admitted publicly that Barbie worked for CIC,

have consistently maintained that no one in CIC knew anything about Barbie's war crimes. They even claimed that if
they had known about them, they would not have employed
him. Capt. Kolb makes a distinction between killing French
resistance fighters and killing Jews. He claims that he knew
that Barbie fought against the French underground, whom
he considered soldiers, but not that Barbie was involved in the
deportation of Jews, whom he considered civilians.

In Augsburg I met Bechtold twice, but we only discussed
housekeeping details; not a word was said about the network.
When I was finally assigned to the U.S. Constabulary Forces
in Stuttgart as a Major in November 18, 1948, I lost track of
Barbie. I heard of him again in September 1949 when he was
still working for the Americans.

Who is the real Klaus Barbie? What were his crimes?

Each of the reports that have now been gathered about
Barbie's crimes and background, substantiates his status as a
habitual prevaricator. He has consistently given false
information about such basic biographical data as his
birthday, place of birth, and date of marriage.

According to the best records and archives available in
Germany, France, and the United States, Klaus Barbie was
born on October 25, 1913, in the city of Bad Godesberg, a
beautiful resort town across the Rhine from Bonn. His father,
at one time an office clerk, later became an elementary school
teacher, whom Barbie referred to as only a "little" teacher.
His father died at the age of 45 as a result of wounds received
during World War I. Barbie reportedly hated the French
because his father was wounded in their country.

From Hitler Youth to Nazi Party member

Barbie attended the high school known as the Frederick-
Wilhelm *Gymnasium* in the city of Trier, graduating in 1934.

Even before his graduation he had joined the Hitler Youth—in April of 1933, just three months after Hitler came to power. He spent six months in the voluntary labor service, that later became compulsory.

Early in 1935 Barbie met Heinrich Himmler, and on December 26 of that year he joined the SD—the *Sicherheitsdienst.* He joined Section IV, the intelligence section, in Berlin. In 1937 he was transferred to Düsseldorf, where records show that he joined the Nazi party in May; his membership number was 4,584,085. In Düsseldorf he met Regine-Margareta Willms, an activist in the Nazi women's auxillary, and they became engaged in 1939. They were married in Berlin on April 25, 1940.

For some reason his new wife was unable to participate in a mandatory course for brides of SS leaders. Barbie had to apologize that she lacked the time. Five days before his wedding he was promoted from noncommissioned officer to second lieutenant in the SS *(Untersturmführer).*

Atrocities begin in Holland

In May, 1940, Barbie was transferred to Holland, which had recently been occupied. There he was assigned to the Jewish command of the SD, first in The Hague and later in Amsterdam. While on duty in Holland he received a promotion to first lieutenant. On April 20, 1941, he was awarded the Iron Cross second class with swords for "cleaning out" a ghetto of 300 Jews. From January 1941 to March 1942, he was active in Amsterdam, where he continued to round up Jews. He was also stationed in Brussels, Belgium, for a short time. He reported to headquarters in Berlin that his wife had given birth to a daughter, Ute Regine, on July 4, 1941, at their home in Trier.

Barbie becomes "SS Hauptsturmführer"

In May of 1942 Barbie was finally transferred to France, first to the small town of Gex, in the Department of the Ain, and then in November 1942 to Lyons, where he headed Section IV—Gestapo and Intelligence. Here he was to pursue members of the French Resistance with the brutal persistence that earned him the epithet "Butcher of Lyons." It has been documented that he participated in the liquidation of a Jewish orphanage; on April 7, 1944, he reported to his Paris headquarters, "mission accomplished." It has also been conclusively proved that in the spring of 1943 he captured a resistance fighter by the name of Kemmler (most likely his code name). He beat him for hours with a big club and then let his men beat him with heavy chains. Kemmler died as a result of Barbie's torture.

The total number of those who died as a direct result of Barbie's actions—who were tortured, shot as hostages, or deported—is unknown. People speak of thousands, as many as ten thousand, who were deported with his help, most never to return. In an interview in Bolivia, Barbie once stated that he didn't know what happened to them in the concentration camps, and that he had heard that many of them had come back.

A French military tribunal found him guilty of deporting 7,500 people, personally participating in 4,342 murders, and arresting and participating in the torture of 14,311 resistance fighters. For these crimes he was twice sentenced to death in absentia; first on May 16, 1947, and again on November 28, 1952. French law prohibits carrying out a sentence passed in absentia without a new trial. Since the death penalty has been abolished in France, life in prison is now the harshest sentence that can be dealt him.

Barbie left Lyons early enough to return to Germany as the Allied forces were pushing the Germans out of France. He was assigned to the SD office in the city of Dortmund. On

November 9, 1944, he was promoted to Captain, or SS *Hauptsturmführer*. After the war his second child, a son named Klaus Georg, was born on December 11, 1946. Klaus was killed in Bolivia in 1980 in a hang-glider accident. In 1968 he married a French girl, Francoise Crozier, who is still living in Bolivia with their three children. Barbie's daughter Ute Regine Messner, a librarian in Kufstein, Austria, is married to a teacher. Barbie's wife Regine died of cancer in 1982. From 1947 to 1951, as has been discussed, Barbie worked for CIC, the American Counter-Intelligence Corps.

5 Two Star Witnesses Eliminated: One Dead, One Missing

Petersen Network and its bosses

Barbie's involvement with Kurt Merk is among the most esoteric chapters of the Barbie saga. Merk, a pleasant-looking young member of the German regular army counterintelligence *(Abwehr)*, participated with Barbie in several major espionage coups in occupied France. He went to work for the American Counter Intelligence Corps (CIC) in 1946. When, in April of 1947, he met Barbie by chance at an Augsburg railroad station, Merk was so well entrenched in CIC's Region IV that he was able to offer Barbie a job. This casual encounter marked the beginning of a top secret intelligence operation conducted for CIC by a team that produced fantastic results. They functioned under the code name of the Petersen Network. Merk had used the name Walter Petersen since the end of the war.

Cherchez la femme

Merk's constant companion was an attractive, auburn-haired Frenchwoman who had helped him penetrate a number of French resistance organizations in 1942 and 1943. She never concealed the fact that if Kurt hadn't brought her to Germany, France would have executed her as a traitor. In order to protect her, Merk provided her with such aliases as Astrid Boehm, Annemarie Richter, and, of course, her real name Andree Simone Rivez, the name by which I knew her in Augsburg.

Merk and his mistress seemed genuinely in love. They made a rather odd-looking couple in that Andree was nearly a head taller than the stocky Kurt. He was always very attentive, and considerate of her needs. He was also keenly aware that by bringing her to Germany he placed himself in a precarious position.

Whenever I could find French magazines and news-papers, I brought them to her. She read them avidly, while lying fully dressed across a carefully made bed. Because she spoke very little German and I had a good basic command of French, she was eager to talk to me whenever I had a chance to visit. She was bored and unhappy, smiling only when Merk came home. "What I didn't do for that man! It is beyond all comprehension," she lamented. "I became a traitor to my country and had to leave—all for the love of a man!"

Andree was carried on a list of sub-informants of the Petersen Network under the name of Annemarie Richter so that Merk could obtain payment for both himself and his mistress. When the couple went out socializing, they were always known as husband and wife. Among Americans with whom he had contact, other than those who were his immediate employers, they were introduced as Kurt and Astrid Petersen. In the house on Mozartstrasse 10, Stadtbergen, a suburb of Augsburg, they were a picture of

Andree Simone Rivez (Merk's mistress) and Kurt Merk
as sketched by Sketch Artist Ken Garrigues.

wedded bliss as Mr. and Mrs. Merk—Kurt and Annemarie.
On several occasions Andree's mother, who was introduced
to me as Mrs. Boehm, although she also used several aliases,
visited her daughter for two week intervals.

A visit to Dinkelscherben

Merk's background is as fascinating as the work he
performed for American intelligence. He was born May 3,
1915, in the small farm hamlet of Fleinhausen, which has
now been incorporated into the village of Dinkelscherben in
the county of Augsburg. Although he was baptized Joseph
Merk, after his father, as a young man of 18 he began to call
himself Kurt, or Kurti. The discovery that he was born out of
wedlock, caused a rift between him and his father. He
refused to use the same first name. Merk's father, Joseph, is
still living in the same pitiful farmhouse where Kurt and
two brothers and sister were born. The living quarters are
dirty and run-down. Chickens and rabbits also have access
to the house.

The old man was born in the same village in 1894, and
looked very much like his son Kurt. His memory is still
excellent. He reads the newspaper without glasses but
suffers from arthritis in both legs. With two homemade
sticks he manages to walk through his little house and yard.

One of his sons, Alfons, was killed on the Russian front in
1942, and the youngest son, Leonard, died March 1983 in
Fleinhausen. The sister lives in a relatively new house
nearby. Her name is Mathilde, after her mother, whose
maiden name was Guggemos. Old man Merk has been a
widower for the past 13 years. His daughter, who is married
to a Czech refugee named Schwellek, brings a meal to him
every day. A grandson, Leonard's son, lives next door to the
old man in a beautifully rebuilt modern house.

The entire community of Fleinhausen knows that something strange has happened to Kurt Merk. Everyone acted

very mysterious when I asked directions to the house of Joseph Merk. I was fortunate to enter the old man's house unnoticed and spend over one hour talking to him; however, when I returned, as I promised him, three days later, I was not permitted to see him. His daughter and the wife of his grandson ordered me to leave the premises.

During my visit the old man only made derogatory remarks about his son Kurt. The Merk family had been cheese-makers for three generations, and he had hoped that his first-born son would continue in the same trade. Kurt had expressed a desire to study for the priesthood, but unfortunately there was not enough money in the family to pay for tuition for the *Gymnasium* (high school).

Suddenly, old man Merk began to reminisce. He remembered his four years during World War I when he was twice wounded. In 1914 he fell in love with Mathilde Guggemos. She was one of three daughters whose parents owned the local sawmill. Before he left for the war he made his sweetheart pregnant. With a twinkle in his eyes he confided, "Joseph, whom you call Kurt, was a child of love (ein Kind der Liebe)."

His steel-blue eyes were shiny when he said, "I told Mathilde, if I do not come back from the war, you will have someone to remember me by." The baby was seven months old before he saw him on his first furlough home from the war. Without hesitation he continued, "I was not able to marry my sweetheart until 1922."

After the usual tour of duty in the German labor service, Kurt joined the army. He had told his father that he did not care to become an officer, so he became a sergeant in the artillery. His father remembered that Kurt told him, "Officers do not make enough money and have to always behave in a correct military manner. A non-commissioned officer can carry more booty home from conquered countries."

However, when Kurt was assigned to counter-intelligence, he was made an officer and ended the war as captain. The father remembers that Kurt visited his home town only a few times during and after the war. He came to see his mother, who spent most of her time at the sawmill with her two sisters. "I only saw my son two or three times during the last ten years of his life. My son knew I had no use for him, his work in intelligence, or his French mistress."

The father saw Andree only twice; once, right after the war in 1945, and the last time, at his son's funeral. Both times Andree's mother was also present, which proves that Merk brought both of them out of France when he returned to Germany. Old man Merk continued, "Andree was no beauty. I believe he should have left her in France."

When I asked him if he thought his son had married his French mistress, he answered without hesitation, "I am sure he did not. He would have had to obtain his birth certificate and other legal documents from the village clerk. I know he never did because the village clerk is a friend of mine and he would have told me." When the father asked Kurt on his first visit in 1945 what he intended to do in the future, Kurt answered that he would probably go to America.

1949: Year of decision for Merk

Despite his leadership role in the Petersen Network, the Ryan Report is quite vague about Kurt Merk, and never mentions his French mistress. In a footnote on page 66 the report states: "Quite apart from HQ's decision, Merk was apparently getting restless in Augsburg. He had some medical problems, he felt constrained by the reduced scope of his net, and tension with Barbie was growing. Merk was inactive during the summer of 1949 because of his medical problems, and he was severed from CIC in October 1949."

Did he move to CIA?

The remaining two years of Merk's life have the makings of a mystery novel. Although CIC dropped him in October of 1949, he continued to work for American intelligence, possibly the CIA, from another location. Merk was still working for the U.S. at the time of his death, probably for the Gehlen Organization, which was organized and controlled by the CIA. The operations officer of Region IV, Capt. Max Etkin. once suggested turning Merk over to the French in order to get rid of him, since Merk and Barbie were no longer getting along. But because it was suspected that the French wanted to use Merk themselves, rather than try him as a war criminal, Etkin lost enthusiasm for releasing such a valuable asset to them. He suggested that Merk might be a good candidate for the CIA instead.

In the fall of 1949 Merk moved—with his mistress and her mother—to the village of Ammerland on Lake Starnberg near Münsing. His entourage no doubt included his sub-informants from the Petersen Network.

Merk's address in Ammerland was Riedhaus 1. A Kurt Westermaier rented the house to Merk from 1949 until his death on September 4, 1951. After Merk's death, the house was sold to the present owner, who completely remodeled it. The address of the house later became Riedweg 27.

Local citizens, for example Mr. Graf, who owns the laundry and dry-cleaning establishment, remember Kurt Merk distinctly. It was common knowledge among them that he worked for an American intelligence organization with headquarters in a large villa, which resembled a small castle, on Lake Starnberg.

Barbie's suspicions confirmed

I am convinced that what had been a simple falling-out developed into a very serious conflict between Barbie and

Merk. Barbie knew that the only real witness to his crimes in France was Kurt Merk. When Barbie was confronted with questions about atrocities that he had committed in France, which he vehemently denied, he felt certain that Merk had been talking. If Barbie could get Merk transferred out of the Augsburg area, he would be the sole leader of the Petersen Network.

Merk, Barbie methods in sharp contrast

Merk was unquestionably the driving force of the network. He had hired Barbie, and the network's code name, Petersen, was the same as Merk's alias, Walter Buro Petersen. It was common practice by American intelligence units to use a non-SS man who had not been charged with atrocities as a front, so that we would be working with a "clean" and reputable man. He might then use war criminals as sub-informants, but the operation maintained a respectable façade.

Merk was by far the more polished intelligence officer; he had achieved his successes with cleverness and finesse. Barbie, by contrast, was known to use brutal torture in order to make his victims talk.

During a two-week period in July, 1948, when Barbie was away at ECIC, Merk worked alone. The quality of material he presented to me for translation was of far greater importance—and substantiated—than the material submitted by Barbie. Merk's sub-informants also appeared to be more intelligent than those used by Barbie—generally former SS officers or black-market operators.

The Ryan Report states that by the summer of 1947, Merk's net of 50 informants operated throughout Germany and much of Eastern Europe. Barbie, as Merk's chief assistant, was given the important job of establishing long-

Merk's last home in Ammerland on Lake Starnberg, where he lived before he was "killed".

range penetration of French intelligence installations in the French Zone. This he accomplished with excellent, ever-increasing results. During my association with these two men, Barbie made every effort to appear as the network's number-one man rather than merely Merk's assistant.

Barbie had a tendency to write his reports in a melodramatic style and was not above copying information from German newspapers in order to embellish them. To him, the game of espionage was a cloak-and-dagger matter. It was not unusual for Barbie to call me out of bed at two a.m. for a clandestine meeting near a railroad underpass with information that could easily have waited until morning. During one of these hastily called meetings, Barbie introduced me to a man who claimed to have just arrived from Baden-Baden, in the French Zone of Occupation. This particular sub-source worked for French intelligence. These informants were of vital importance to Barbie personally; it was critical that he keep abreast of the efforts the French were making to locate him.

Merk's excellent connections with former German intelligence officers produced a great quantity of key information for CIC. He certainly deserved as much U.S. help as Barbie received. Why then were he and his French mistress not allowed to disappear into South America?

Merk's mysterious demise

It seems reasonable that Barbie was able to convince his American superiors that Merk's departure should be denied. The likely scenario: Barbie learned from one of his American handlers that Merk had in fact talked to me about his war crimes in France. He then, before his own departure, arranged with one of his former SS buddies for Merk's demise.

In March, 1951, CIC finally helped Barbie escape to Bolivia by way of the "rat line." Only one witness remained in Germany who could attest to Barbie's activities in Lyons. Less than six months after Barbie was safely out of Europe with his wife and two children, that witness—Kurt Merk— died at the age of 36 under extremely unusual circumstances.

His death certificate, filed in the town clerk's office of the village of Münsing, states that Kurt Merk died on September 4, 1951.

Christian who?

His death was reported at 4:50 PM by a Christian Hettich, a truck driver who claimed to reside in the village of Tutzing, directly across Lake Starnberg from the village of Ammerland. A search of the village records at Tutzing provided the unusual information that no one named Christian Hettich had ever resided in that town.

The clerk at the town office ran the name through the computer under various possible spellings. We tried Hättich, Hättig, and Hettig with the same negative results. There is no doubt that the man who reported Merk's death was never a resident of the town of Tutzing.

Who was Christian Hettich? Perhaps he was a co-worker of Merk, employed by the Gehlen Organization in Pullach near Munich, or an American CIA agent. The town of residence for this mysterious truck driver was probably chosen because it was located immediately across the lake, and residents of Tutzing would not generally be known either in Ammerland or Münsing.

Merk's death certificate says that Kurt Merk was born May 3, 1915. His father is listed as Joseph Merk, his mother as Mathilda Merk, nee Guggemos, and his birthplace as the town of Fleinhausen, now Dinkelsherben, in the county of

Kurt Merk's father in the living room of his house in Fleinhausen, posing for the author in October 1983.

Kurt Merk's father on his home made crutches in front of his farmhouse in Fleinhausen, photographed by the author in October 1983.

Augsburg. He is recorded as having been married to Astrid Merk, nee Richter. In the margin of the death certificate is a notice from the circuit court in Munich, dated September 20, 1951, to the clerk's office in Münsing to correct the death certificate by striking the word "married" on line 11, because Kurt Merk was not married.

"No comment!"

A local physician who now lives at Hoherrainerstrasse 6, had viewed Merk's body and signed the death certificate; at the bottom of the page he listed the cause of death as sudden heart attack *(plötzlich Herztod)*. It is known both in Ammerland, where Merk died, and in Fleinhausen, where he was buried, that his oak coffin was purchased by Americans, and that Americans transported his body to his father's house in Fleinhausen, on September 5, 1951, the day after his death. The burial took place that same day and his coffin was never opened. All funeral expenses were paid by the Americans.

In February of 1983, a German journalist who heard my report about Barbie and Kurt Merk over Radio Bremen, began investigating the Merk connection. He discovered that a woman in Augsburg, our network's former secretary, received a call from an American unit informing her of Merk's death. She drove to Ammerland, where she saw the doctor examining his body in the presence of his French mistress, who was then using the alias Astrid. At the time of his demise, it was rumored that Merk died as the result of a wasp sting. The people in Merk's home town believe that rumor to this day. Our secretary, after seeing Merk's body, distinctly remembers having seen a small dark blue spot behind one ear, a spot not unlike that made by a small-caliber bullet.

Merk's father also believes that Kurt Merk died of a wasp sting. Why then did the physician inscribe sudden heart death on the death certificate?

Photo of Walther 7.65mm Pistol, believed to be the type of weapon used to inflict the deadly "bee-sting" behind Merk's ear. Its small calibre and enormously powerful velocity explain why such a bullet wound could easily be mistaken for a bee sting.

During a visit to Münsing, I attempted to talk about Merk to the physician, who has a flourishing practice there. Knowing that NBC had been unable to interview—or even photograph—the good doctor, and that he refused to talk to reporters, I decided to visit him during his office hours. When his receptionist asked whether I had been there before, I replied, "No, this is my first time. I'm just traveling through town and have a sore throat. I would like to see the doctor."

The nurse asked me to wait in another room. A half-hour later the doctor appeared, saying, "What seems to be the trouble?"

I immediately identified myself and asked, "Doctor, would you be good enough to clarify some misconceptions about Merk's death? Do you know the woman who was living with him at the time of his death, or where I might find her? I'm not questioning your diagnosis that Merk died of a sudden heart failure, but I would like to know why so many people believe he died of a wasp sting."

Gesticulating wildly, the doctor tried to stop me from talking. He screamed at me, "I will not talk to anyone! I have said everything I'm going to say regarding the Merk death. I want no further involvement and I am ordering you to leave this room immediately!"

Why would this seemingly reasonable gentleman of some 65 years, whose medical reputation is above reproach, refuse to discuss the untimely death of Kurt Merk? Is he worried about his original diagnosis of sudden heart attack? Has he been told by someone to keep his mouth shut? Did he "miss" the bullet hole behind the ear? Does he know where Merk's mistress is today?

It is inexplicable to me that a respected doctor would refuse to talk to anyone unless he has something to hide. Is it possible that the people who paid his bill had urged him to forget this particular case? It is strange indeed that no autopsy was requested by the German authorities and that Merk's body was buried one day after his death. If, however, Merk was still working for the Americans, as his father had indicated, it is not unlikely that the CIA wanted no publicity about the mysterious death of one of its star performers. When the doctor pointed his finger at the door and ordered me to leave his premises, I had the distinct feeling that I had stirred up a hornet's nest.

Barbie burns his bridges, Rivez vanishes

Merk was constantly concerned about protecting his French mistress. With the French closing in on Barbie, it was more than prudent of Merk to leave the Augsburg region to avoid compromising her safety. But, even in far-away Bolivia, Barbie was anything but comfortable about having this witness to his atrocities living in the beautiful foothills of the Bavarian Alps and working for the Americans. And Barbie was hardly above having informants eliminated; he had extensive experience along these lines.

In late December of 1948 or early January of 1949, my technical specialist, Richard K. Lavoie, reported that British intelligence was looking for Barbie. They were concerned that Barbie might be organizing an effort to "eliminate" Germans who spied for the British. Lavoie said, "I knew of Barbie's hatred for the British because of his alleged mistreatment by them during his brief arrest and imprisonment in 1946, but I had satisfied myself that Barbie was not actually trying to eliminate British informants."

I had worked with the British during the war and my experience makes it difficult to understand why Lavoie believed Barbie's allegations of mistreatment. Lavoie never indicated how he had satisfied himself that Barbie

SECURITY

APO 407 - a

Operations
18 February 1948
From: EUCOM
Ref. Nr. 6148
Group Count 21

The following purportedly INFORMANTS of CIC are wanted by the
French War Crimes: LT MERCK German connected with ABWEHRSTELLUNG
in Stuttgart; MLLE ANDREE RIVES; PECQUIGNOT mother of RIVES. Request
immediate notification of present whereabouts of same. Desire immediate
notification of the existence of same and the veracity of allegation.
Cite Vidal SECRET Signed ERSKINE

Decoded by Foehl

*This secret cable was sent from European Command to CIC Region IV
on February 18, 1948. This proves that several members of CIC
prevented the extradition of Merk, his mistress Andree Rivez, and her
mother Mrs. Pequignot. The Ryan Report claims that no members of
CIC knew that the above informants were wanted for war crimes by
the French until May 1949. This cable clearly shows that CIC was
informed that the French requested immediate notification of the
whereabouts of these three informants. Merk's network was already on
the CIC payroll for over one year when this request was received.
There can be no doubt that a real cover-up existed.*

was not eliminating British informants. I can only assume that he asked Barbie, who would certainly have denied it.

Lavoie also said that he passed this information on to Joseph Vidal at CIC headquarters in Frankfurt to find out what he should tell the British about Barbie. Vidal decided, apparently on his own, that, "Since British intelligence had not asked CIC directly for information on Barbie, there would be no reply until we are asked specifically."

This was a most unprofessional approach in view of the fact that the U.S. owes much of its intelligence training to the British.

On my first meeting with Kurt Merk, in Kempten in the summer of 1948, he had proved to me that he was a loyal German espionage agent. He explained, "When you guys," referring to the American army, "kicked us out of France, I naturally could not leave my informants behind. That would mean certain execution. You should have seen me crossing the Rhine river back into Germany. We looked like a gypsy caravan. I was driving a large truck with a live-in trailer attached, loaded with all kinds of people who had worked for me in France."

Although the Ryan Report briefly mentions that CIC headquarters believed that the French were looking for Merk, during my tour of duty with CIC, I never came across Merk's name on a French wanted list. They were certainly looking for Barbie. If the French were in fact looking for Merk, it was probably because of his mistress.

Why no one in CIC bothered to look into Merk's activity in France and that of his mistress Andree Rivez is highly unusual and difficult to explain. Apparently no one wanted to disturb any French relationship in order to protect Barbie. Little did anyone know that Merk was not even on the wanted list in France but his mistress certainly was. Not only did we protect a known Nazi war criminal, Klaus

Barbie, but a well known French traitor whom **Merk** was protecting, Andree Rivez.

Merk arrived in France as an *Abwehr* agent in November 1940. His first assignment was with French custom officials in the Colmar region not far from Freiburg, Germany, and he had soon established an important network of French agents and collaborators.

In February of 1941 he was assigned to the city of Dijon. There he began working with Andree Rivez and with her help accomplished some of his famous intelligence successes in 1942/1943.

Andree was born in February 1915 in Valdoie, a suburb of Belfort, France, and she had worked as an informant for the Gestapo in Strassburg since 1938. This was only one of several secret Gestapo offices in France which the Germans set up and used to develop sympathizers and expand their fifth columns. This proves that Hitler was preparing his attack on France long before May 1940 by establishing many pro-Nazi enclaves prior to the actual invasion.

Andree's mother's maiden name was Merlen. She was married to a man named Rivez when her daughter Andree was born. She later divorced him and married a man with the name of Pequignot. Andree became very friendly with her uncle Merlen, her mother's brother, who in 1942 was police commissioner of the city of Lyons. Andree was briefly married to a man named Jean Louis Boehm but after her divorce, she again only used her maiden name. When Merk met Andree in 1942 in Dijon, she became his mistress, and through her was able to penetrate the French police and intelligence organization in Lyons, by turning her uncle into a collaborator. As a result of Merk's action with the help of Andree, 84 French collaborators were arrested and sentenced in Dijon to various prison terms. Seven of the French collaborators were sentenced to death, the uncle was executed and Merk's most valuable paid informant, Jean

Paul Lien, was also executed. Andree Rivez was sentenced to death in absentia, but Merk had done a good job of protecting her in Germany, with the help of CIC.

After Merk's death, Andree Rivez seems to have vanished. If she's still alive, for all I know she might be among my neighbors in Grosse Pointe, Michigan. I wonder if she will decide to write me a little note.

Merk's legacy of "achievements"

Merk told me on several occasions of his fantastic espionage successes. In 1942-43 he had infiltrated and neutralized the National Liberation movement of the Resistance in Dijon, with the help of his mistress. In Lyon, with Barbie's help, he nearly annihilated the French intelligence office (2 éme Bureau). His master stroke was the destruction of the intelligence source known as *Alliance*. Merk told me that he was glad that he had not had to do the dirty work. The arrests and deportations of his French targets were carried out by the German military police and the French Gendarmerie. In Lyons, Barbie's special SD command performed the gruesome tasks. "All I had to do was point out the locations, and write the reports; the repugnant details were left to other organizations."

As a valued informant for CIC for many years, Merk in all probability obtained a reasonable contract as a CIA consultant. This contract certainly included funeral expenses; did it also include life insurance with which his family was able to rebuild his sister's house?

6　Barbie Not The Only SS Chief On U.S. Payroll

K laus Barbie was not the only war criminal or high-ranking Nazi officer employed by American intelligence. When I arrived in Stuttgart on November 19, 1948, I went to the headquarters of the U.S. Constabulary, located on the out skirts of the city in a large former German barracks called the Vaihingen *Kaserne*. This Constabulary, a special border unit drawn from former U.S. Army Armored Divisions, patrolled the border between U.S. and Russian occupied territory. It is interesting to note that although the Russians were still our allies and we were continuing to supply them with lend-lease equipment, they were already mining their side of the border and beginning to build the "iron curtain," first with barbed wire and then with other fortifications. I was introduced to Major Charles Hiatt, who said, "Major Dabringhaus, I'm glad to have you aboard. You're now officially a member of the 7827 MIS (Military Intelligence Service). We are part of the U.S. Constabulary forces in Germany."

"I'm very glad to be with you," I replied. "I just left a very delicate assignment in Augsburg where I was control officer of a special network of informants run by Kurt Merk and Klaus Barbie. What is your general mission?"

"The U.S. Constabulary controls the border between East and West," Hiatt explained. "One of our primary missions is to interrogate border-crossers for strategic intelligence of the Soviet Zone and Czechoslovakia. But since you have had experience with informant networks, I think I'll assign you to a very important group of informants composed primarily of former SS officers. During your work you should wear civilian clothes and only appear in uniform during official functions here at headquarters."

A well-run intelligence unit

Unfortunately Major Hiatt had no knowledge of either Merk or Barbie, and therefore he could not comment about them when I mentioned my previous assignment. Although Major Hiatt was a West Point graduate, he was unable to communicate in German, nor had he any prior intelligence training. Nevertheless, he was a topflight administrator and deserves much of the credit for the excellent and efficient operation of our unit.

We operated from a requisitioned house in the middle-class suburb of Degerloch. No American families lived nearby; our neighbors were all Germans whose backgrounds had been checked out in previous years. Two of our agents, Master Sergeant Glaubitz and Technical Sergeant Hohensee, were non-commissioned officers who spoke excellent German. A first lieutenant and a corporal handled the administrative duties of the safe house.

The smooth operation then in progress was impressive. The staff of the unit immediately began briefing me regarding the overall mission. In Augsburg the CIC agents were never properly briefed, and no one trusted anyone else. We three special agents frequently discussed the operation and shared information with each other. Whenever the Constabulary patrols picked up a border-crosser, they delivered him to our Degerloch house for extensive interrogation. Any valuable information produced was properly recorded for higher headquarters.

After a brief training period, agent Glaubitz took me to another safe house operated by our MIS detachment. It was located in the city of Ludwigsburg, just a few miles from Stuttgart. The safe house had three floors. The leader of the network lived on the top floor in a fully equipped apartment. There were four small apartments on the second floor and two large units on the ground floor. The first and second floor apartments were then vacant, but showed signs of recent occupancy.

Glaubitz explained that the house was designated as an American-requisitioned billet, totally restricted for our use. Informants were occasionally housed on the second floor if we needed to hold them for further interrogation. "The third floor is off limits to everyone except you and me," Glaubitz said. "Those quarters are now occupied by SS Col. Gunther Bernau, who heads our network of SS informants. Now that you are taking over this network, I'll give you my key to his apartment. Only you and Bernau will be permitted to enter."

A soldier and a gentleman

"Bernau has produced some fantastic information for us," he added. "As you establish your relationship with him as the American leader of the network, I'll be glad to tell you all I know about him. However, I think you should take over in your own style."

"Let's go upstairs and meet the s.o.b.," I said.

"Just a minute!" Glaubitz retorted, "This guy is valuable stuff. We treat him like a gentleman."

We knocked on his door; the colonel opened it. I was presented to Bernau as the new control officer. After a few minutes of small talk, I suggested that we meet the next morning and get down to business. It was obvious that this was a professionally run operation, a far cry from the intrigues I had experienced with the Merk-Barbie Network in Augsburg.

The following morning Bernau and I got acquainted. He was a handsome man in his late thirties, tall and athletic with a wiry build that reflected his years of hard soldiering at the front line. He would have been perfectly type-cast as a Hollywood version SS officer. When he learned that I was a major in the army with five campaigns in Europe and the Normandy invasion under my belt, his respect was immediate. He unhesitantly recounted his own war experiences.

He had been a regimental commander in the 5th SS Viking Division, which had been committed to the Eastern front. He was quick to point out that his division was the only one exonerated in Nürnberg of all war crimes. "We were constantly in the front line," he said, "and were never used in rear areas to round up or execute Russian partisans."

A failure to fire

He had clearly enjoyed his years of war-time duty. His closest call had come fighting in a Russian village under close-combat conditions. "I was almost a goner," he said with excitement in his voice. "I stepped out of a house into the back yard. At precisely the same moment a Russian officer stepped out of the house next door. We faced each other with our pistols drawn. We pulled our triggers simultaneously. The hammers clicked, but neither pistol fired. I was the lucky one. I pulled the trigger again, and the bullet hit the Russian officer. He had taken a second longer to eject the old bullet, pull the breach back, and reload. Just as his bullet went off, he fell dead to the ground."

Bernau was very proud that he had followed the proper procedure when his pistol failed to fire. "If I had not done so," he observed, "I would not be here today."

Bernau moved through the apartment with light, springy steps, showing pride in his physical fitness. He never denied that he was a good Nazi. He belonged to a large organization of former SS officers who were prepared to fight even after the war was over. As he matter-of-factly told me the following day, "If soldiers become buddies in the foxholes on the front line during the war, they become even greater friends behind barbed wire in internment camps. You Americans put all of us SS men together after the war, according to the automatic arrest category."

Brüderschaft (Brotherhood)

Bernau and his fellow inmates had spent only five weeks in a camp near Darmstadt, but their stay was long enough for them to swear eternal friendship. The SS network of informants was founded on an oath to Hitler and loyalty to each other. Their brotherhood, which included the elimination of undesirable witnesses or informants was to continue for decades. Klaus Barbie, who had been a leader of the network, was able to direct it even from faraway Bolivia.

During his internment, Bernau, who was not charged with any crimes, offered the services of his SS friends to American intelligence for a price. He claimed that he could mobilize a group of 200 former SS officers with one telephone call to Hamburg. His most valuable assets were informants in the Soviet Zone of Occupation; he claimed to have contact with sub-sources as far away as Moscow.

Bernau's network, which had begun working for various American intelligence units in 1946, had been under the Constabulary control for only a year. When I told Bernau that I had been working with Klaus Barbie, he informed me that they were good friends. Between the end of the war and the summer of 1946, the two colleagues had attempted to form their own neo-Nazi organization. Their men had buried small arms weapons in the redoubt area of the Bavarian and Bohemian Forests in South Eastern Germany, near the Czech border. Bernau gave me the location of this cache and we were able to confiscate the entire supply. Its location was neatly marked on trees. The weapons, protected by cosmoline grease, were buried in 25 large holes, each containing approximately 100 Walther, Luger, and P-38 pistols and sub-machine guns, plus thousands of rounds of ammunition.

Theirs was a highly clandestine resistance effort. "Although I was originally in charge of the military arm of the organization," Bernau told me, "I soon convinced my associates that it was totally impossible to operate on the basis of violence or terrorism."

Instead of military opposition, Bernau suggested developing large intelligence networks and offering them to the British and American occupation forces. In return, in addition to the usual supplies of cigarettes, coffee, and ration cards, the SS informants would be allowed to assume responsibility for the German administration of towns throughout the American and British Zones. This system would provide a strong, experienced corps of post-war leaders not only loyal to Germany but, of greater importance to U.S. and British occupation forces, solidly opposed to communism.

An S.S. network is formed

The occupation leaders agreed to accept the network's offer and the SS organization functioned exactly in this manner for many months—until the allied occupiers realized that the scheme was primarily designed to protect the thousands of SS men still living illegally in Germany. These men—known war criminals—were hiding with false identification.

When my division fought through the town of Schwarzenbach, *an der Saale,* most of the male population had not returned. Our military affairs officer was only able to find a former concentration camp inmate to appoint as mayor. In December, 1945, I passed through Schwarzenbach on my way to visit my wife in Belgium. I stopped to see how the mayor was getting along in his job. I was surprised to find that the former concentration camp inmate, a Social Democrat, had been replaced by a former SS officer who had recently been cleared of war crimes and returned from an internment camp. When I questioned this, I was told that the erstwhile mayor was unqualified and that the former SS officer had far more administrative experience. I reported this to my headquarters but was told that this was not considered to be a security threat. Similar occurences were commonplace in villages and towns all over Germany.

Bernau remembered that Barbie's alias was "Klaus Becker" and that within their intelligence organization his speciality was the procurement of money, radio equipment, and printing presses. Barbie boasted to Bernau that he had learned to forge nearly 300 different documents, which he then provided to friends who were still living illegally.

The SS operation is broken up

In February of 1947, British military intelligence, in conjunction with CIC, decided to break up this clandestine organization. It was a well-planned sweep to capture as many SS as possible for detailed interrogation. CIC executed this sweep on February 23 under the code name "Operation Selection Board." The names and addresses of suspected SS organization members—Barbie's included— were provided to British and American intelligence as targets of the operation. The sweep, which took place in the early morning hours, netted nearly 70 persons, who were arrested and detained for interrogation. Barbie, however, eluded capture. An inside tip apparently enabled him to avoid detection and resurface in the vicinity of his old friend Merk, who then recruited him to join the U.S.-sponsored Petersen Network.

The virtual destruction of the clandestine SS net brought Barbie and Bernau to the realization that it would be better to cooperate with the Americans than to oppose them. After 1947 both men became paid informants of U.S. intelligence. In a truly spectacular blunder—which graphically illustrates the depth of inexperience of our own intelligence agents—one region of CIC was ordering Barbie's arrest when another region had already "carded" him as a paid informant.

I had been working with Bernau for several weeks when I recognized some material that he had submitted as valuable information. It was a report that I had already received from Barbie three months earlier. It referred to the location of a uranium mine that the Russians were working in the Soviet sector of Germany near the town of Aue. At that time the Russians did not yet have the atomic bomb. This piece of information was therefore of enormous significance, since the Russians did not explode an atom bomb until August, 1949.

When Barbie was officially recruited, he had promised to break all ties with his former SS friends. When I confronted Bernau with my discovery, he readily admitted that some of his informants had maintained contact with Barbie during the previous two years. The fact that different American intelligence organizations were repeatedly paying for the same pieces of information several times over, was apparently never noticed by the evaluators since each unit guarded its intelligence so jealously.

Wartime memories

One day Bernau was late for one of our frequent appointments, so I let myself in with my key. While waiting for him to show up, I glanced through a bookshelf in his living room and came upon a picture album, of his wartime experiences. I took down the album and it fell open at the middle. A large picture of Hitler, which covered the entire page, stared back at me. At that moment Bernau entered the room and saw that I had the album on my lap and was looking at the picture of the *Führer*. Flustered, he began to speak, "Major Dabringhaus, you must not think me ungrateful or disrespectful to the Americans because I keep the picture of Hitler in my album. But when you hold your head against a brutal enemy for four long years for the *Vaterland* and your *Führer*, it is very difficult to cast those years aside in a short period of time."

I said, "Colonel, you have no need to explain your reasons for keeping his picture. I understand your emotional involvement, but I hope that it will not interfere with your present loyalty to the American forces in Germany. After all, four years have passed and you must now think about your future."

I meet SS General Hausser

After this encounter, Bernau was even more open about his activities, and the reports I was sending to my headquarters began to have substantive information about the Soviet sector of Germany. One day he introduced me to SS General *(Obergruppenführer)* Paul Hausser, who had commanded the German 7th Army in Normandy. In the final collapse of the Normandy campaign, Gen. Hausser had been seriously wounded. He now had difficulty walking and his face was badly disfigured.

Bernau explained that Gen. Hausser was one of the highest ranking SS officers to survive the war. Bernau occasionally supported Hausser with food and money since he was unable to adequately take care of himself—another example of the sworn brotherhood created in the internment camps. At this meeting with Gen. Hausser, I realized that he had been a frequent visitor at Bernau's apartment.

SS colonel invites me to his wedding

From that moment on Bernau took me into his confidence regarding his assistance to his former SS buddies. One day I was introduced to a former regimental commander of the 12th SS Panzer Division, *Hitlerjugend,* who was still living under an assumed name. He humbly explained to me, "I come from a fine Prussian family in Bremen and have fallen in love with a beautiful girl from Vienna. We are planning to get married, but I hate to get married using an alias. That would destroy my family tree. The rub is that my name still appears on the 'wanted' list, and I have been afraid to come out of hiding. Would you be good enough to find out why I am on the wanted list? As far as I know, I have not committed any atrocities."

I searched at ECIC and found that the only reason the Americans wanted this former SS officer was to ask him to report to Bad Homburg, where our historical division was located, in order to record his recollections of his campaigns in Normandy and during the Battle of the Bulge. When I gave the colonel this information, he jumped for joy. He left for Bad Homburg the next day, and six weeks later he invited me to his wedding, which I of course declined.

When, in May 1949, the new Federal Republic of Germany was formed by the union of the three western occupation zones, many of Bernau's informants gradually returned to civilian employment in government and industry. Some also found employment in the *Gehlen Verein* which the U.S. supported. This organization later became the *Bundesnachrichten Dienst* of the new German Federal Republic, which is the German counterpart to the U.S. Central Intelligence Agency.

Since my own former 1st U.S. Infantry Division was still on occupation duty in Germany, I requested transfer to that division. I turned my command back to Major Hiatt and Sgt. Hohensee took charge. On May 6, 1949, I became the Assistant Chief of Staff G2 of the division in Bad Tölz, Germany.

7 Barbie Fails To Turn Hardy Into a Double Agent

Col. René Hardy, a well-known French Resistance fighter, was primarily in charge of blowing up railroads. He had been prosecuted in 1948 and again in 1950 by the French Government for alleged collaboration. The most serious charge against Hardy was that he had arranged the arrest of France's most honored resistance fighter, Jean Moulin.

Jean Moulin had been savagely beaten by Barbie and had died on route to Germany; his body was then brought back to Paris for cremation. Much later in 1964, his ashes were transferred to the resting place of many French heroes, the Panthéon. During the ceremony, de Gaulle's good friend, André Malraux, described the revered Resistance leader as "the champion of the people of the night."

Our government investigation alludes briefly to the fact that the French entered the picture in 1948, but only to obtain information about Col. Hardy. There are several dates given on which the French were permitted to interrogate Barbie concerning the actions of Col. Hardy. Two of the meetings took place on May 14 and 18, 1948, shortly after Barbie's release from the ECIC. There are no American documents referring to these interrogations by the French, but France has records of them, which are kept in the Archives of the Ministry of Justice.

French ask, "Where's Barbie?"

French agents twice quizzed me as to the whereabouts of Barbie. The first time, a hurried meeting followed an urgent phone call from Captain George M. Spiller, who was my immediate administrative superior in the Sub-Region of Augsburg. With excitement in his voice he said, "There are two French agents on their way to your office. Get rid of Barbie and Merk and tell the agents that you don't know anything about Barbie!"

The two gentlemen were very polite. I told them that I didn't even know the name Klaus Barbie, and was greatly surprised when they failed to press me for additional information. They gave no hint of what they had in mind or why they were looking for Barbie. We chatted about wine and champagne.

Approximately four weeks later I was asked to come to Munich. This time two different officers from the French Government showed up to ask me whether I knew where Klaus Barbie was. Again I had been told by Col. Golden, who was in charge of the region, to say I knew nothing about Klaus Barbie. Again the French officers made no mention of the fact that Barbie was a war criminal—that they were looking for him because of his crimes during his stay in France. The U.S. government's official investigation of these events (the Ryan Report, discussed in detail in Chapter 8) indicates that the French wanted Barbie only as a material witness for the second Hardy trial. In his first trial Hardy denied ever having been captured by Barbie.

If the French had in fact interrogated Barbie, why was I asked to deny any knowledge of him? The only plausible answer is that I was to throw the French off the track as to where Barbie was working in order to end their search for him. The French were not satisfied with Barbie's testimony and wanted him to appear at Hardy's trial in Paris. French agents continued their attempts to locate Barbie.

Lieutenant John Whiteway, a Canadian citizen serving as the French liaison officer to the European Command (EUCOM), approached CIC and requested that the French be given permission to take Barbie to Paris. A verbal request for Barbie to appear at the trial in Paris arrived at about the same time. CIC was reluctant to release Barbie even if promised that he would be returned to the United States Zone of Occupation following his appearance in Paris. Barbie had often said, "If I ever fall into the hands of the French, I will be executed."

All CIC members involved with the Barbie operation undoubtedly knew of Barbie's fear. Nobody ever asked why Barbie was afraid to go to Paris.

Barbie finally testifies

Although the CIC brass were unwilling to release Barbie for the purpose of being a witness, Lieutenant Whiteway and the technical specialist at CIC Headquarters in Frankfurt finally agreed to let French officials return to the U.S. Zone to take Barbie's testimony. On January 21, 1949, French officials interrogated Barbie about the Hardy case in Munich, in the presence of CIC officers. The Ryan Report specifically states that nothing else was discussed. The French did, however, return on two other occasions in early 1949 to question Barbie in greater detail.

It is obvious from the Ryan Report that my two visits from French agents were totally unofficial—that they had not been cleared through our headquarters. It would naturally follow that the French were on Barbie's trail and that they hoped to arrest him and take him to France, not only as a witness in the Hardy trial, but to stand trial himself for war crimes.

Sureté penetrated by communists?

The fact that the French were sending all kinds of agents into the American Zone to learn the whereabouts of Barbie appears in a footnote on page 69 of the Ryan Report:

> "During this time, CIC was also concerned and annoyed by the quite separate efforts of the Sureté, the French National Police, who were sending 'various and sundry individuals' into the U.S. Zone to seek information, from German police and CIC agents in the field, on Barbie's whereabouts. CIC Headquarters was convinced that the Sureté at that time had been 'thoroughly penetrated by communist elements' who wanted to kidnap Barbie, reveal his CIC connection, and thus embarrass the United States. According to CIC technical specialist Vidal, CIC was by now 'even more desirous of protecting Barbie,' and Vidal complained to Lieutenant Whiteway that the Sureté should 'follow channels,' by routing any requests through Whiteway. Lieutenant Whiteway apparently agreed with the CICs characterization of the Sureté's motives and tactics and he reportedly agreed to correct these 'irregular approaches.'"

The basis for Agent Vidal's statement that the French Sureté was thoroughly penetrated by communist elements is not at all clear. It probably came from Barbie. Jealousy among our Western Allies had become increasingly visible. Loyal Americans wanted to protect the United States from the communist threat. The McCarthy era was only a few years away.

What convinced our CIC operations' officers that these "various and sundry individuals" came into the American Zone to annoy or embarrass the United States? Didn't anybody realize that the French wanted Barbie to face the music for war crimes?

I was never told that the French had been authorized to interrogate Barbie in Frankfurt in 1948 concerning the Hardy affair. Barbie apparently had been instructed not to mention it to his American agent. The hush-hush surrounding the meeting was that of a cloak-and-dagger scenario in which someone in higher headquarters was playing a major role. Many officers saw both the need and the opportunity to expand CIC into an ambitious political operation. Unfortunately, the frequent lack of intelligence experience left them unprepared for the sinister world of spying.

Barbie turns journalist

After Barbie had been interrogated by French agents, he returned one day from a visit to Munich and decided to write down his recollections of Col. Hardy's arrest.

He dictated to his secretary in our office for several hours. When she had typed some six or seven double-spaced pages, he called me and said, "Dabringhaus, would you please sell this story to an American newspaper? I need the money."

The Merk-Barbie Network was always in need of money and Barbie always wanted American dollars. I took the article home with me and carefully read what he had written. His story contained some startling revelations.

It began with Barbie hanging on the outside of an overloaded streetcar in Munich, where the passengers resembled "a bunch of grapes hanging on the vine." As the streetcar passed a large kiosk, he noticed a German newspaper headline referring to Hardy's first trial, in which the

Colonel had denied ever having been arrested by the Germans. This lie prompted Barbie to write his version of the event so that the world would know that he, the best intelligence chief in France, had brought about Hardy's arrest. His vanity was clearly wounded, which I believe gives his statements considerable credence.

Whether Barbie's article, which I read carefully several times, contained the same information he had given to the French interrogators cannot be verified because their reports are missing. But it is probably different. If he had told the French agents the same story, why would he now bother to write it down?

Barbie began his description of the arrest of René Hardy, who was high on his list as a candidate to become a double agent, by pointing out that he had been looking for him for several weeks. He finally arrested Hardy on a train, somewhere between Dijon and Lyons.

According to his version of the episode, Barbie drove Hardy to his headquarters in Lyons. After a night of forceful interrogation, Barbie thought that he had nearly broken Hardy's spirit. Barbie relaxed his interrogation in hopes of turning him into a double agent. Barbie told him to think it over and said he would get back to him later.

Barbie also mentioned something about a technical office used by Hardy and British intelligence agents as a cover. Barbie repeated the word "Technica" over and over again, and said that he believed Hardy was connected with it, possibly as one of its leaders. Barbie had learned that the Office of Technica was located in Rouen, which meant that for the first time, Northern France was now, a target for counter-espionage.

Hardy strolls to freedom

Convinced that the British were in charge, and that through Hardy he might penetrate "Technica," Barbie was relatively easy on Hardy. The next day he permitted him to walk around the building and talk to other people. His plan, which was to obtain Hardy's cooperation through psychology rather than force, was unsuccessful: Hardy was able to walk right past the guard at the door and make his escape. Barbie not only insisted that he did not release Hardy, but that he was furious, beating up the guard for letting Hardy leave as if he had been a visitor rather than a prisoner.

Barbie's article did not mention the Jean Moulin story. Had Hardy actually been the informer in the case of the meeting on June 21, 1943, in Caluire, Barbie would certainly have included that fact.

Hardy with an "H"

A major factor in Barbie's conviction that Hardy worked for British Intelligence was his name. A German, like an Englishman, would pronounce Hardy with an "H," and not "Ardee," as the French would say it. Barbie never knew Hardy's cover name, Didot.

He explained to me after giving me the article that if he had penetrated Technica with the help of Hardy, he certainly would have received a promotion. He had primarily operated against resistance organizations in Lyons, and to have penetrated British Intelligence in Northern France would have been worth at least another decoration. Barbie then exclaimed, "I could go to Paris and exonerate Col. Hardy of any collaboration with us. But I cannot afford that. I would not come back alive."

Why was Barbie's story withheld from the French?

I carefully translated Barbie's article and sent it up to my headquarters, but made no effort to sell it to an American newspaper. Since CIC had already given the French permission to talk to Barbie, it is a mystery to me that this information was not turned over to France. Because I was already giving him a considerable amount of money, I just told him I would see about it. I put the article among my personal papers.

While I was assigned to the First U.S. Infantry Division as Assistant Chief of Staff, G2, this same Barbie story was suddenly mentioned again. It was in September, 1949. My immediate superior, Col. Myron Tauer, the G2 of the Division, called me into his office, and in a very hush-hush manner said, "Major Dabringhaus, what do you know about Klaus Barbie?"

Startled, I answered, "I know a lot about Klaus Barbie. I worked with him as a member of the CIC in Augsburg last year."

"That's interesting!" he responded. "I have an order here to ask you whether you are still in possession of papers that belong to Klaus Barbie."

"That is the strangest request I ever heard. I had no reason to keep papers that belonged to Klaus Barbie. Who wants to know, anyway?" I retorted.

"I cannot tell you that," he said, "but it is very important. It comes from a very high echelon. You are supposed to have sold a story for Klaus Barbie, and he never got the money."

I then briefly explained my experience with Barbie to Col. Tauer and outlined Barbie's story of the Col. Hardy episode. I had never offered to sell it to anybody and told the Colonel that it was probably still among my papers at home.

Quick! Find the manuscript!

He then ordered me to leave for home right away. "It's very urgent! Look for it! I've got to have it! Somebody in higher headquarters is asking for it."

I immediately drove to my house, where, amidst my papers, I found Barbie's story—written in German and entitled something like *"How I Captured Col. Hardy on a Train in France."* Col. Tauer seemed very relieved that I had the article and dismissed me after I handed it to him.

I have no knowledge of what office or headquarters asked for Barbie's story, and cannot now ask Col. Tauer as he passed away several years ago. The incident does, however, indicate that Barbie was still working for CIC in Germany at that time. It also indicates that Barbie was under the impression that I sold the story to an American newspaper without reimbursing him.

The story of Col. Hardy by Klaus Barbie is nowhere to be found in the U.S. Department of Justice Report, nor in the official apology to France submitted by the U.S. in August, 1983. It was probably among those documents that were destroyed after being submitted and analyzed; a fantastic case of obstruction of justice! It could have made an enormous difference in Col. Hardy's second trial, which did not take place until 1950.

Barbie wrote his story for publication for two reasons: money, and because Hardy, in his first trial, had denied that he had been captured by the Germans. Barbie's pride was wounded, especially since Hardy had been acquitted in the first trial. Barbie wrote a detailed account of how he had caused Hardy's capture on a train to Paris.

Moulin knew that Barbie was closing in on him. He had sent a message to London on May 7, 1943, indicating that Vichy and Nazi secret agents were hot on his trail. He blamed poor security among certain leaders of the Resistance. Three days after he issued an order, he told London, the Gestapo had a copy of it. He found this out from one of his spies at Gestapo headquarters. A meeting of Resistance leaders scheduled by Moulin for June 21, 1943, in Caluire, a suburb of Lyons, was to be his last. It became the scene of Moulin's infamous capture.

Hardy was the only resistance fighter to escape. The meeting was set for 2 p.m. at the house of Dr. Frédéric Dugoujon, who is today the mayor of Caluire. Moulin arrived at 2:40, and at 2:45 Barbie and his gang showed up. Mysteriously, there was no outside Resistance security placed around the doctor's house. This laxity was particularly strange in view of the importance of the meeting. This normally routine precaution might have saved Moulin's life.

Moulin had earlier expressed concern about a lack of discipline among the Resistance leaders. If Hardy had in fact been the traitor to betray Moulin by exposing the meeting to Barbie, he could easily have arranged not to be on hand for his capture. Several of the invited leaders did miss the meeting, claiming that they could not find the doctor's house. It was true that anyone not familiar with the hills surrounding Lyons could easily have lost his way.

There were rumors that the French London headquarters had been responsible for Moulin's betrayal because they feared he might become a serious rival to General de Gaulle. If Barbie had succeeded in turning Hardy into a double agent, he would certainly have disclosed the fact that Hardy was the tip-off man. Such a damaging revelation would have made Barbie's journalistic effort much more saleable.

After Hardy's initial escape from Barbie's detention, Hardy made sure that he was seen in the presence of many Resistance leaders between June 10 and June 20. Had Hardy been released by Barbie as a double agent, he would have been followed and his contacts arrested. None of them were. It is known that Hardy continued to work on behalf of the Resistance by blowing up railroad tracks, trains, and stations, until he and his fiancée made their way to North Africa.

The fact that Hardy alone escaped from the June 21 meeting in Caluire has kept his innocence under a shadow of suspicion. Because he was the only one to escape and merely shot in the arm, it is frequently assumed that the Germans allowed him to get away. Yet if Hardy's bizarre escape had been planned by Barbie, this aspect of Hardy's collaboration would have been a focal point of Barbie's article, which instead emphasized that Hardy had never collaborated.

Finally, Barbie never knew who of the Resistance leaders was actually Jean Moulin until he had been beaten at Gestapo headquarters, where his identity was finally revealed. He had been brought to Barbie's prison as Jean Martel, a patient who was consulting the doctor about his rheumatism. On the afternoon of June 23, Barbie learned from a stool pigeon in the prison that the patient-prisoner Martel was really Max, the code name for Jean Moulin. If Hardy had fingered Moulin, he would, as a matter of course, have given Barbie an accurate description of the famous leader of the Resistance, as a good double agent should. Barbie's identification of the hero of the Resistance would then have been immediate, instead of taking two days.

The final bizarre element of the Barbie-Hardy relationship emerged from my questioning by Richard D. Sullivan, of the U.S. Attorney General's Office of Special Investigation. During the five-hour interview that Sullivan conducted in my living room (which is discussed in Chapter 8), he asked me, "Does the word 'Technica' mean anything to you?"

I was very surprised, and responded "The only time I ever heard the word 'Technica' was in Barbie's story about Hardy."

Sullivan made no mention of the source of the name and simply dropped the subject.

Ryan Report omits Barbie-Hardy link

Surprisingly, the Ryan Report contains no reference to this particular organization or to the Barbie and Hardy relationship. The only reference to the Hardy story is a comment by committee Chairman Allan A. Ryan, Jr., about a book called *Soldiers of the Night*, by David Schoenbrun, which documents Hardy's participation in the French Resistance. Instead of giving information on what he might have found in the documents, Ryan simply refers the reader to Schoenbrun's excellent report on the French Resistance.

Hardy's innocence is clear

I hope that I have been able to shed some new light upon "L'Affaire Hardy" and to correct the false assumptions of those in France who may still consider him to have been a traitor. Barbie's story disproves that. Barbie has become a more-than-competent liar, but back in 1948, while working under the protection of the U.S. Army CIC, he had no reason not to tell the truth. If Hardy *had* been the tip-off man about the meeting, Barbie would have included this fact in his article. It would have made his account far more attractive to a prospective buyer, and he had written the story for the express purpose of selling it.

Col. Hardy's second trial, which took place in 1950, ended in a hung jury. According to French law, Hardy has thus legally been found innocent. But because in the eyes of many Frenchmen Hardy's absolute innocence has never been established, it is my hope that this additional information helps prove that Col. Hardy is clearly and unequivocally not guilty.

Col. Hardy, now 73, lives in Normandy. When asked by reporters whether he was willing to testify in the Barbie trial, he said yes without hesitation. When it was disclosed that Barbie was living in La Paz, Bolivia, Hardy volunteered to meet him face-to-face. Efforts to negotiate such a meeting ensued, but Barbie refused to meet Hardy.

U.S. Department of Justice

AARyan:jdo
146-2-47-KB

Washington, D.C. 20530

August 17, 1983

Dear Mr. Dabringhaus:

    I am enclosing a copy of the report that was released
yesterday by the Department of Justice on the Klaus Barbie
investigation.

    I appreciate your assistance in this investigation.
Please do not hesitate to contact me if you have any questions
or comments on this report.

                  Sincerely,

                  Allan A. Ryan, Jr.
                  Special Assistant to the Assistant
                   Attorney General
                  Office of Special Investigations
                  U.S. Department of Justice
                  Criminal Divison
                  Suite 195
                  1377 K. Street, N.W.
                  Washington, D.C. 20005

Enclosure

8 Justice Department and Congressional Aides Check My Story

On Monday, February 7, representatives of American and Canadian newspapers, radio, and TV stations began calling. Many interested journalists were digging into archives for further information. I also received a phone call from the U.S. General Accounting Office (GAO) requesting an appointment for a John Tipton to come and interview me. When I asked who John Tipton was, the GAO staff member replied, "He works for the intelligence Committee of the House of Representatives."

I made arrangements to meet with Tipton at his convenience. He arrived on February 13 with an associate. We spent an hour discussing the employment of Klaus Barbie. During our conversation Tipton said, "For many years we've been investigating the fact that many Nazi war criminals have entered the United States illegally, sometimes even with the help of American intelligence agencies. I am a senior evaluator of the Congressional Intelligence Committee, which is chaired by Congressman Peter W. Rodino, Democrat from New Jersey, who is also chairman of the House Judiciary Committee. We were instrumental in finding several high-ranking Nazi officials who have been permitted to immigrate to our country. Several of these people had their citizenship revoked and we're still looking for countries that will accept them."

Tipton was the first member of a governmental organization to contact me after the news hit the air waves. He was also very polite and indicated that my information might prove useful, and that he would contact me at a later date.

Ten days later I received a letter from Tipton in which he thanked me for the interview and enclosed a copy of the latest report on Nazi war criminals issued by the GAO, which is the watch dog of the U.S. government. This report, issued in 1978, shows a thorough investigation of those people who lied about coming to this country or who had been helped to come to this country by some of our intelligence agencies, which is why Tipton was interested in the involvement of the American Counter Intelligence Corps with Klaus Barbie.

Soon after I met Tipton, I was contacted by Peter Sullivan, representing the Select Committee on Intelligence of the United States Senate, whose vice-chairman is New York Senator Daniel Patrick Moynihan. "I am a legal advisor for the committee," he said, "and am interested in the connection between Klaus Barbie and intelligence agencies."

Loftus and "The Belarus Secret"

Another interesting call came from John Loftus, an attorney in Boston, who is the author of *The Belarus Secret* (Knopf, 1982). This book deals with Russian immigrants who came shortly after the war, and were employed by some of our American intelligence agencies.

In June, 1941, the Germans began their campaign against the Russians under the code name Barbarossa. The German armies immediately found a great number of Byelorussians who welcomed the Germans with open arms. These Byelorussians were politically opposed to Russia's communist regime and consequently were willing to support the German Army in its drive against Russia. They even formed an SS division. When the war was over, they couldn't stay in Russia since they had participated in many atrocities against their own people and the Jews. They moved into Germany with the help of the German Army and offered their service to the Americans.

We learned that the Byelorussians despised the communist system and we considered them a valuable ally in the struggle against communism. Many of them were used as spies in Soviet-occupied territories. When this network was penetrated by Soviet agents, the survivors were smuggled into the United States.

Loftus had asked whether I knew anything about the cover office of the State Department for which Klaus Barbie might have worked. This intelligence office was known under the title of Office of Policy Coordination. One of Loftus' important arguments, which he thoroughly documented and vehemently pursued in *The Belarus Street,* was the use of former Nazis by this highly secret State Department intelligence group. It is not clear, however, whether Barbie ever had any contact with the Office of Policy Coordination.

Media interest intensifies; death threats received

The Barbie story had created unprecedented interest throughout the world. Many well-known national and international journalists called or came to the house. Many investigative reporters called me to verify names and places and refresh my memory. Pat Tyler of *The Washington Post,* Ralph Blumenthal of *The New York Times,* Robert Shackney of CBS News, John Martin of ABC News, Robert Fink of BBC News, and Walter Karpf of *Stern* Magazine's New York

Office are among those who were generous with their information and suggestions. It was an exhilarating experience, but highly time-consuming and at times very fatiguing.

Some of the telephone calls were unnerving. One man called me a *Schwein,* then said, "If you can't speak or understand German any more, that means pig in English. If you go to France to testify, you're a dead duck."

I also received several threatening letters. One of them had me in a grave with my name printed on the tombstone. Although I suspected that these were cranks, my local Grosse Pointe Woods Police Department thought them serious enough to add surveillance on our house.

We have a very good security department in our city. One morning a limousine was to pick me up to appear on the "Today" show. The driver was actually stopped entering my street. A police officer in an unmarked car escorted him to my house and verified that I was expecting a limousine.

Even at the University a plain-clothes security officer accompanied me everywhere. These precautions continued for several weeks. Then the momentum of the news gradually diminished and we were able to continue a slightly more normal life. A truly "normal" existence, however, is not yet in sight; we continue to get nuisance or annoyance calls almost every night. Whenever there is any reference to Barbie in the media, my phone begins ringing in the middle of the night. When I finally get up to answer or stop the ringing, the caller hangs up. On those nights we go to sleep with the phone off the hook.

The Barbie story is turning into a landmark case. What has the world learned from the events of Hitlerism? About half of my German-American friends called me soon after the story broke and said, "We are proud of you." and "It takes a lot of guts to tell the truth." But the other half weren't so sure. They implied that I should have kept my mouth shut. "Why get involved in something that happened so long ago?"

My coming out with the story has in some instances been misconstrued. One hate newspaper published in Manhattan Beach, California, known as *Truth Mission*, put me on their mailing list. They thought I was a good anti-Semite. The copy that they mailed me had nothing but hate stories denying the Holocaust. They figured I was protecting Barbie by implying that he worked for the United States and I was on his side.

Forgive and forget?

Many of us have tried very hard to forgive what happened during the Nazi regime, but never to forget. Today, a large percentage of the population apparently would like to do both—forgive *and* forget.

Most soldiers on both sides of the war conducted themselves in a proper manner but the murder of prisoners or children, even in wartime, should never have statutes of limitations placed upon it. Some of our own citizens will say "forget" because 35 years have passed; the time gap is too great. Yet, if you commit murder in the United States, no time limitation will save you from prosecution.

In France the trial is certain to revive old memories. It will also help youthful French men and women—and children—understand what this traumatic period was like and why it should not be forgotten. If we do not learn from history, we are condemned to repeat it.

U.S. Attorney General orders investigation

On March 15, 1983, the Attorney General was finally asked to investigate my allegations concerning Klaus Barbie. He turned the assignment over to the Office of Special Investigations, under the chairmanship of Allan A. Ryan, Jr. The pressure to investigate had come primarily from Jewish organizations. Israel's Prime Minister Menachem Begin, who was in the U.S. during that period, is believed to have convinced the President to order the investigation.

On May 19, 1983, Richard D. Sullivan, a trial lawyer by profession and a member of the Office of Special Investigation, arrived at my home. My first impression was less than favorable. Sullivan immediately began to browbeat me by suggesting that my memory, after three decades, couldn't be that good. He implied that I had fabricated much of the story. Standing my ground, I replied, "Why don't you get the records from the CIC? They must be available in the archives. I recently learned that after you opened the investigation, you reclassified all the documents in the National Archives. They are all of a sudden Top Secret again and no one can get to them. I hope you have access to these records!"

Very calmly Sullivan replied, "I certainly do! I have them all, right here in my briefcase. There are several of us on the committee, and we are looking up every American agent who had any contact with Klaus Barbie. Ryan and I were in Bolivia a couple of weeks ago. That's where we began our investigation."

I asked, "Why didn't you contact me sooner?"

He responded, "We wanted to save you for last since you broke the story in the first place."

After a few hours Sullivan became friendlier and told me of some of his experiences in Vietnam in the Marine Corps. After he showed me some documents proving that my memory was indeed good, the final hour of our discussion was quite amicable. He acknowledged that my memory was exceptionally good and I convinced him that there are a few events in a man's life that are unforgettable; one, when he first meets his future wife, and two, when he finds out he's working with a Nazi war criminal.

He showed me several documents, including a letter with my signature which contained items of information that were totally unfamiliar to me. It is very possible that this letter was written by my technical specialist, Lieutenant Richard K. Lavoie. Sullivan pointed out that Lt. Lavoie was in charge of the network in my Munich headquarters. The letter was probably prepared by Lavoie with information that I had passed up, and signed by me after a cursory glance. (This procedure was well known in the service. We normally never hesitated to carry out our superior's requests. I signed virtually any document prepared for my signature.)

According to this document I was supposed to have picked up Klaus Barbie on June 15, 1948, along with five other people. This to me is totally incomprehensible since I distinctly remember moving only Klaus Barbie, Kurt Merk, and his mistress Andree Simone Rivez from Kempten to Augsburg. The letter Sullivan showed me is dated June 18 and states that I also took Andree's mother and Dr. Emil Augsburg and his female secretary.

I was driving a three-quarter-ton Dodge truck that my good friend Sammy Denato, our motor pool Sergeant, had readied for me. I had only three people in that truck—not six. Barbie came to the front and sat in the cab with me, while Merk and his mistress and all the heavy suitcases and boxes were in the back of the truck. Three more people certainly would have stuck in my mind. The other three moved themselves into the safe house several weeks later.

Sullivan badgered me for approximately four hours. He agreed that Barbie had been working for us. He further volunteered that an agent by the name of Herbert Bechtold took over after I left in November of 1948. In 1949 another agent took over; his name was Eugene Kolb. Barbie worked for CIC for four years, after which we helped him reach Bolivia.

I said, "Mr. Sullivan, if this is true, how are you going to explain that we shielded him, protected him, and helped him to escape to South America when the French were looking for him?"

He replied, "It is a tricky situation and we have some embarrassed people who might well have broken the law. But you must remember the United States is a powerful government. We might call a grand jury and some of the people involved with the cover-up could go to jail unless the statutes of limitations are up. Some of the documents we have in our possession will hold up in a court of law."

He then explained, "We have several options that we could use. The first option is, in the interest of National Security, to just deny everything. When your story first came out, you may recall that the standard answer used by the State and Justice Departments was "no comment." In our second option we would claim that Dabringhaus had a stroke, became senile and lost his memory, and what he said was all wrong. The third option would be to tell the truth. And lastly we could urgently impress upon the French government that they ought to take more stringent actions against Barbie."

This statement almost knocked me over. I wondered aloud, "Mr. Sullivan—you wouldn't do that, would you?"

"You have no idea what we would do. We could do almost anything," he replied with a grin. "We are a powerful country."

I then retorted, "The reason I actually came forward with this information was to set the record straight and tell history factually. This is no longer classified information, is it?"

He replied, "Yes, that's true. I understand your reason. I feel very confident that you had no ulterior motive. We know your record. I have your military record right here in my briefcase."

"Oh that's where it is!" I exclaimed, "I just got a letter from the National Military Personnel Records Center in St. Louis, Missouri. They said that it had been returned to the originating agency."

He said, "We are the originating agency. When this investigation is over, we'll be glad to forward it to you under the Freedom of Information Act, as you previously requested."

I asked Sullivan, "How long would it take for the investigation to be terminated, and would you make the findings public?"

He answered, "That all depends on the members of the committee. As you know, Mr. Ryan is the chairman, and whatever he decides in collaboration with the Assistant Attorney General will determine the end result."

Although Sullivan was smiling when he remarked that we would ask the French to eliminate Barbie it is becoming increasingly clear that the public is often kept in the dark about national policies. In my view it would be wrong for our government to deny this story or to deny the truth about American involvement with Klaus Barbie.

At about 4:30, we shook hands, and he said, "You will hear from me if I need more information. Otherwise, you can expect the report in three to four months."

9 Whitewash!!!

U.S. apology to France and
what the Ryan Report did not reveal

On August 15, 1983, the United States Department of Justice announced that a report covering U.S. government involvement with Klaus Barbie would be released in a few days. Allan A. Ryan Jr., Special Assistant to the Assistant Attorney General, headed the investigation. When the media received the 218-page report on August 17, the resultant uproar was nearly as great as that of February 5, 1983, when I first announced that Barbie had worked for the United States after the war.

Ryan and his committee are to be commended for issuing their voluminous report in record time. We can take pride in the fact that our government saw fit to examine the hundreds of relevant documents and make its findings available to the public. On a personal level, I was, of course, pleased that these findings generally corroborate my earlier statements.

U.S. apologizes to France

It is a tribute to the strength of our democratic process that the report urged an official apology to the French government. In voicing the U.S. Government's regret, Ryan pointed out that "Justice delayed is Justice denied."

The committee's goal, as Ryan notes in his introduction, was to determine the truth and report it. I wonder whether any other country in the world would take the step of publishing a similarly comprehensive report of such a profoundly embarrassing episode.

After thorough study of the Ryan Report, I find that I must question some of its conclusions. The report also leaves room for considerable speculation about documents that seem to be conveniently missing.

CIC members withhold information

There is no question that several CIC members either lied to their superiors or withheld information from responsible government agencies for periods of up to six months. The chaotic conditions under which the United States Army had to operate in postwar Germany and the inexperience of many of our CIC agents were among the factors responsible for mistakes made by some of our military personnel.

In answering the question, "Was the Army justified in using Barbie after the war?", Ryan relies on both pragmatism and emotionalism, which are mutually exclusive.

As discussed in Chapter II, the practical reason for using Klaus Barbie after the war is that Russia, who had been our ally during the war, had abruptly become a military and political adversary. Ryan concludes that there was a legitimate need for the United States to recognize, understand, and, where necessary, counteract Soviet actions. The Soviets represented a serious threat to the American occupation in Germany and to the interests of the Western Alliance.

It was a major blunder for many CIC personnel to forget that France was our ally. Jealousy was clearly a problem among allied occupation forces in Germany, but to imply that French intelligence forces, if not the entire French government, had been penetrated by communists was a feeble excuse for the continued use of a guy like Barbie. Yet the belief was widespread. One CIC officer actually remarked on television not long ago that "If we had turned Barbie over to the French, he would have been in Moscow a few days later."

No one in CIC was soft on Nazis, but replacements who had not experienced the war often had little knowledge of the military and political climate of postwar Germany. And it is important to note that we had received a directive from higher headquarters to the effect that after June, 1948, we were to turn our attention from former Nazis to the communists.

Ryan makes this statement in his conclusion: "If a Klaus Barbie was available and effective and loyal and reliable—and those who worked with him found him to be all of those—his employment was in the best interests of the United States at that time."

As one of those who worked with him, I did indeed find him available and effective, but never loyal or reliable. It is obvious that CIC should have requested a thorough investigation of Barbie's entire background from ECIC, rather than of just his activities from 1945 to 1948. Had they done so, they would have discovered that Barbie, particularly in his role as the Butcher of Lyons, was far too sadistic and depraved to be considered as a potential U.S. informant.

Barbie's past conveniently covered up

One of the Ryan Report's most glaring omissions is its failure to deal with the disappearance of my reports of Barbie's war crimes. How could detailed information about Barbie's acts of torture and murder, reliable reports given to me by his close associate, Kurt Merk, *not be forwarded to higher headquarters?* Agents who served after I left contended that they knew nothing of Barbie's atrocities in France until they were featured in a Paris newspaper article on May 13, 1949.

How could I have been the only agent handling the Petersen Network able to obtain information about Barbie's monstrous past? The Ryan Report emphasizes the fact that I led the network only from June to October of 1948, and that the other agents worked with Barbie for longer periods of time. Was I a better interrogator than the other agents, or did I have a closer working relationship with Merk and Barbie? Although these factors may have helped determine how *much* I learned about his past, I have a sneaking suspicion that all reports about Barbie's war crimes were suppressed by eager technical specialists who wanted to keep Klaus Barbie on board as a key U.S. informant.

SD most vicious SS units

The United States and its allies had waged war against the Nazi regime in Europe for nearly four years. More than 200,000 American lives had been lost. The Nazis had become the most vicious political power in history. They had murdered—well behind the lines of combat—more than 11 million innocent victims. Of these, 6 million had been systematically exterminated simply because they were Jewish.

The SS had been the instrument of slaughter, operating the death camps and doing most of the killing behind the lines. Barbie's organization, the SD, were the most brutal units of the SS. It was also, in many ways, the most important segment of the German government. During the last three years of the war the SD worked directly with Hitler and Himmler to run the government.

The SS was designated a "criminal organization" at the Nürnberg War Crimes Trials in 1946. Their weapons were terrorism, torture, and murder. As Ryan justly states, "To actually employ a man who had been a leader of the hated SD in a city in France, and to rely on him to advance the interests of the United States, was incomprehensible and shameful."

Ryan implies that each argument is compelling in its own fashion: the pragmatic judgment draws its strength from looking to the future, and the visceral judgment draws its strength from looking at the past.

It is truly unfortunate that the investigators were persuaded that CIC personnel had no reliable indication until May, 1949, some two years after Barbie's hiring, that he was suspected of war crimes or crimes against humanity. Their conclusion makes it clear that my own reports of the crimes committed by Barbie in Lyons must have been destroyed. The information given to me by Kurt Merk, the personal friend and associate who had hired Barbie in the first place and was an eye witness to his atrocities, was real and verifiable. A footnote from page 55 of the Ryan Report gives credence to my belief that my reports were destroyed:

> *"Verification of the scope of Barbie's operations is difficult in 1983 because the reports filed by him, Merk, and the other informants could not be located and many have been destroyed long ago, 'perhaps shortly after they were submitted and analyzed.' The most reliable present-day guide to this operation are the contemporaneous accounts of CIC's agents handling Barbie and the Merk net, which are quoted in this report. The possibility that even these accounts*

*may be somewhat inflated cannot be overlooked,
however, since they were primarily written to justify
continued employment of the net."*

Barbie's past goes undetected at ECIC

During Barbie's lengthy internment at ECIC—from
December 1947 to May 1948—not one of the interrogators at
this most famous intelligence center of the European
Command learned the truth about his background. They
had been instructed by CIC not to delve into his wartime
activities. This unpardonable action was a conscious effort
to avoid losing him or compromising his status as an
informant.

One of the ECIC interrogators commented, "Barbie is
ready to return to Memmingen to continue with his work.
He prefers to do so, if at all possible, but he is also willing to
transfer to another location or to any other department of
the CIC." He also observed that "Although Barbie claims to
be anti-communist, it is felt that the main reason for his
great effort and endeavors to work for the Western Allies is
based on a desire to obtain his personal freedom. Barbie
falls under the "automatic arrest category" and his present
employment with CIC offers him personal freedom, the
liberty to be with his family, a decent wage, an apartment,
and security. If Barbie were interned," the ECIC interrogator concluded, "he might escape and turn to French or
British intelligence with his extensive knowledge of CIC
operations." All CIC officers were bent on precluding this
possibility.

Report virtually ignores Merk

The Ryan Report glosses over the role of the Petersen
Network's other leading member, Kurt Merk. His French
mistress, Andree Rivez, is not even mentioned. Why doesn't
Merk, who was firmly entrenched as an informant for CIC

Region IV and who was the man responsible for bringing Barbie into the U.S. fold, have a prominent spot in this official report? Merk produced by far the most important intelligence for the Region before he was suddenly ordered dropped from the network whose code name bore his own alias, Petersen.

On April 11, 1949, some nine months after the network began its operation in Augsburg, CIC Headquarters formally notified Region IV that the request for further extension of the net itself was disapproved; no further explanation was given. Col. Browning ordered that Merk be "dropped," but that Barbie continue to be employed, "primarily for the purpose of recruiting informants." This step was to mark the end of Merk's active service to CIC and the demise of a network of informants that at its peak had extended throughout Germany and most of Eastern Europe. But the network was not finished, nor, apparently, was it intended to be. Barbie's services as a full-time employee of the army continued until he was sent to Bolivia in 1951.

The final brief reference in the Ryan Report to Merk's activity is found in a footnote on page 66. "Quite apart from headquarters decision, Merk was apparently getting restless in Augsburg; he felt constrained by the reduced scope of his net, and tension with Barbie was growing. Merk was inactive during the summer of 1949 because of his medical problem, and he was severed from the CIC in October 1949. He died in Germany in 1951." This is another example of where the Ryan Report is deadly wrong. The simple fact is that Merk was in excellent health, and was merely complaining of not having enough work to do. Could it be that Barbie reported this "health" report to higher headquarters, so that he, Barbie, could be the boss? There is circumstantial evidence, described elsewhere in this book, that Barbie may well be responsible for Merk's ultimate demise.

If, as the report states, CIC simply dropped Merk and his mistress in 1949 after they had spent three years producing some of the most important information gathered by the United States in postwar Europe, why wasn't Barbie simply dropped in a similar manner once his value had diminished? Even a cursory investigation of Andree's background in France would have revealed that, like Barbie, she had been sentenced to death in absentia. If Barbie had "earned" the right to be sent to Bolivia, it would seem that Merk and Rivez deserved the same consideration.

The report further states that I was mindful of the French situation in which Merk was involved. This was construed by the investigators to mean that Merk was being sought by the French. They concluded their comments by stating that Merk could easily be controlled by offering him the protection of the U.S. Army. This was a totally incorrect assumption by the technical specialist, or whoever read my report, since I had stated that Merk had never been on the wanted list in France. But the French no doubt knew by then that Merk was protecting the known traitor Andree Rivez, his mistress.

The incredible confusion that prevailed at CIC during my assignment to the Petersen Network is vividly described in the Ryan Report. On August 23, 1948, my technical specialist, Richard Lavoie, responded to a memo from Col. Browning, dated May 28, Lavoie requested approval of our employment of a reorganized Petersen Network. I had been working with the net since at least June 15. How is it possible that the operations officer, Col. Browning, of the headquarters of the CIC has to wait three months for an answer to his memo, and on top of that is told an outright lie. We never stopped using the network. It is also interesting to note that Lavoie's August 23 memo received no reply from headquarters until October 25. The fact that memos between headquarters and regional headquarters went unanswered for several months seems a clear indication of the confusion—or indecision—generated by the all-important question of whether to continue using the services of a known war criminal. Although at that point in the summer of 1948, no one at CIC, the Ryan Report contends, believed that Barbie was wanted for war crimes.

The jealousy with which each region of CIC guarded and controlled its informants is evidenced by an inquiry involving an accusation forwarded from one of the regional headquarters to CIC headquarters: the Merk-Barbie net, working out of Region IV, was, they complained, interfering with its informants and generally invading its territory.

If it is in fact true that until May of 1949 everyone at CIC headquarters believed that Merk—not Barbie—was wanted by an allied country, it becomes obvious that my reports of Barbie's atrocities in France never reached our headquarters in Frankfurt. It also follows that they must have been destroyed at our regional headquarters.

To disregard this critical information about Barbie's past was certainly a direct cover up. Someone in my regional headquarters did not want it known that Barbie was wanted for war crimes because they wanted to continue to use him.

The proposal from headquarters to finally drop the network, or turn it over to the CIA, did not go over at all well with regional headquarters in Munich. On November 16, 1948, the regional operations officer had stated that the reduced network was then quite workable. Merk and Barbie insisted on working as a team; neither wanted to work alone.

Network payroll: Dollars or D-Marks?

The Ryan Report goes to great lengths to contradict my recollection that the Petersen Network received 1,700 American dollars monthly. Many of those contacted during

the investigation claimed that CIC never used American
Dollars. Because I had not seen real dollars for more than
two years, that amount made a vivid impression on me. The
report claims that the net was only paid in marks, food-
stuffs, ration cards, and cigarettes. I know that I saw a
manila envelope stuffed with 1,700 American dollars, and
that Barbie had remarked, "This is our monthly payroll." I,
of course, had no way of knowing whether the envelope containing the money came from CIC or from the black market.

Between April of 1947 and June, 1948, when I took over,
the report claims that the network's monthly payroll ranged
between 7,000 and 15,000 Reichsmarks which at that time
was equivalent to between 700 and 1,500 dollars.

In June of 1948 Germany underwent a currency change.
The old Reichsmark was discontinued and a new Deutsche
Mark, or D-Mark, was introduced. The ratio of the new D-
Mark, a strong currency backed by American dollars,
became a little over 4 D-Marks to the dollar.

At that point many arguments arose between Merk and
Barbie and our technical specialist about their monthly
payroll. The records cited by the Ryan Report show the
monthly payroll to have been comprised primarily of
supplies, valued at 3,500 D-marks, plus some small amounts
of currency. Merk and Barbie insisted that they be paid in
regular American green dollars; otherwise, they said, they
would have to exchange the supplies into American
currency on the black market. I reported to Lavoie that
Merk and Barbie demanded a payroll of 8,000 to 10,000 D-
marks—roughly $2,000 to $2,500—to operate their net
efficiently.

Merk and Barbie needed regular dollars in order to pay
their informants who were living outside of the German
economy. Barbie had also mentioned that many of his
former SS buddies were living in South America and that
in order to get out of Europe he would need real American

dollars. He was no doubt putting some of them aside for his future escape.

It seems totally unreasonable that CIC chose to support the black market by paying its informants largely in supplies which they then had to convert into dollars. A carton of cigarettes, which cost Americans a dollar at the Post Exchange, went for $25 on the black market.

I was sharply reminded of the black-market value of cigarettes while having lunch at a field officer's mess in Frankfurt in December, 1948. As a tip for the German waiter, I was about to leave a pack of cigarettes on the table near my plate, a pack which had cost me ten cents. A lieutenant colonel seated opposite me alerted me to the fact that my gratuity was overly generous. "Please, Major, one or two cigarettes is the normal tip for the waiter in this mess hall; if you leave a whole pack you are overpaying him twenty times and ruining things for the rest of us."

All of our agents received a monthly payment, a "payroll," which was always distributed by our technical specialist to Merk and Barbie, who in turn divided the money among their sub-sources. Records of the distribution of monies and supplies were kept at regional headquarters; the technical specialist was the only one who knew the exact amounts allocated to the network.

The investigation's heavy emphasis on the amounts of these payrolls may reflect efforts to soft-pedal the use of taxpayers' money to reward known war criminals. If Merk's requests for a $2,000 to $2,500 payroll were in fact met, whether in supplies, D-Marks, or dollars, the caliber of the information they produced probably made the money a good investment. In any event, it is ironic that on the one hand the MP's and CID were working to stop black market activities while on the other hand CIC was promoting them.

~~CONFIDENTIAL~~

HEADQUARTERS
AUGSBURG SUB REGION
COUNTER INTELLIGENCE CORPS REGION IV
7970 CIC GROUP
EUROPEAN COMMAND

30-1 52

APO 407-A
13 July 1948

FILE NO: IV-A-1300/64

SUBJECT: Status of Informant Kurt MERK X-3067-IV-K and Sub-Sources.

TO : Commanding Officer, Region IV, 7970 CIC Group, APO 407-A, US Army. (ATTN: Lt. LAVOIE, Operations).

1. Reference is made to request from Operations Section, Headquarters Region IV pertaining to present status of informants net PETERSEN. On 4 June 1948 the undersigned Agent was requested to take-over the direction of above named informant and 15 June 1948 the first contact was made in AUGSBURG. The undersigned Agent has visited SUBJECT five (5) times in KEMPTEN and presently status of informant is substantially as follows:

a. SUBJECT informant has presently eleven (11) sub-sources under his direction and all personal data concerning these sub-sources will be submitted as soon as the undersigned has agreed to keep them under SUBJECT's direction.

b. Several of his sub-sources have apparently been compromised and are no longer productive. SUBJECT informant has been ordered to de-brief and drop all compromised sources.

2. A house has been secured for SUBJECT informant in AUGSBURG. This house is located at #10 Mozart Strasse, Stadtbergen, AUGSBURG, on the outskirts of a dependent community and has been condemed for occupancy for US personnel by Post Headquarters. SUBJECT informant will occupy above quarters on or about 15 July 1948.

3. Only persons essential to the successful operation of SUBJECT informant's net will be brought into new address in AUGSBURG. These people include SUBJECT, SUBJECT's common-law-wife, mother of wife, and one secretary, and Dr. AUGSBURG and secretary. This involves six (6) persons in all.

4. SUBJECT's sub-source ▓▓▓▓ has been approached by the undersigned and he will be directed separately as of 15 July 1948. ▓▓▓▓ has two (2) sub-sources named ▓▓▓▓ The sub-sources ▓▓▓▓ have each three (3) informants which is the complete net of SUBJECT's sub-sources ▓▓▓▓

5. Since the currency reform on 18 June 1948, SUBJECT informant has not produced any reports with the explanation that all his sources are without funds and unable to travel. On 29 June 1948 the undersigned paid SUBJECT five hundred (500) GERMAN Marks to continue operation. SUBJECT, however, indicated that he would need eight thousand (8000) to ten thousand (10000) GERMAN Marks to operate his net efficiently.

6. It is the opinion of the undersigned that SUBJECT can be of continued value to this organization if his net is directly and closely controlled by the undersigned Agent. All sub-sources should be personally known to the undersigned and all personal data regarding them must be available to this headquarters. Due to the FRENCH situation in which SUBJECT is involved by reason of his association with his present common-law-wife, SUBJECT can be easily controlled by offering him protection of the US Army. The undersigned Agent therefore requests permission to direct SUBJECT informant's net in the manner described above. All new developments will be reported immediately.

Erhard Dabringhaus
ERHARD DABRINGHAUS
Special Agent CIC

2   2
1   6

- 2 -

No mention of my transfer request

The report also makes no mention of the fact that I asked to be transferred when I found out that I was working hand-in-hand with a war criminal; it simply states that I was transferred. If, as Lavoie reported, the great job we were doing resulted in my getting a promotion, what was the reason for my transfer? There is absolutely no answer to this question in the Ryan Report.

It is more than likely that Barbie complained about my handling of the network after I became very cool toward him, and that to appease this war criminal and keep him happy, another agent, Sgt. Herbert Bechtold, was given my place on October 1st. This is a further indication that neither Bechtold nor I were "in charge"—that Barbie was the real CIC agent. I was called back to active duty as a major as of November 18, 1948, which necessitated resigning from CIC; I was not transferred, as stated in the report.

U.S. faces fewer shocks at Barbie trial

If I had not exposed Barbie's involvement with American Intelligence, the Justice Department would not have had to carry out their extensive investigation of the affair nor would an official U.S. apology to France have been necessary. However, when Barbie goes on trial in Lyons, he will certainly clarify the extent of his American connection and the fact that CIC helped him get to Bolivia.

Barbie, who knows my name as well as I know his, is likely to cite the names and activities of many former CIC agents. I believe that it is in our best interests to have this information publicly aired before the trial in Lyons. We, in this country, would have been far more shocked and concerned had Barbie himself been the one to accuse the United States not only of collaborating with him but of shipping him off scot-free to a prosperous new life in Bolivia. To tell the truth... Barbie is no "doll."

10 Barbie Spends 32 Years In Bolivia, Now Awaits Trial in France

After I left the Petersen Network in October, 1948, both Barbie and Merk continued to serve the U.S. Army in various fashions, Merk and his mistress left Augsburg at the end of 1949 for Ammerland, on Lake Starnberg, where they went to work for the CIA and the Gehlen Organization. Following Merk's untimely death on September 4, 1951, his mistress and her mother vanished.

As this is written, Andree is rumored to be living in the Cologne area. Barbie remained in Augsburg in a CIC safe house; in the summer of 1950, he moved his wife, daughter, and son there from Trier. Barbie's value to CIC at that time is highly questionable. The Ryan Report claims that his primary job was to obtain informants. Yet it was known that by this time virtually everyone in Germany, at the insistence of the French government, was looking for Barbie.

CIC knew that our own Public Safety Branch of the U.S. High Commissioner's office, the German police, and Frence Sureté agents were combing the U.S. Zone of

Occupation for the Butcher of Lyons. He told his case officer, "I'm living in constant fear of being apprehended by the French."

The "Rat Line" decision

In December, 1950, CIC headquarters decided to help Barbie and his family make their way to South America. In Austria, a sister organization known as the 430th CIC volunteered to help the Barbie family escape. The 430th CIC had been involved for several years in helping defectors and informants from the Soviet Zone of Austria leave Europe. Their "customers" included many high-ranking Nazis and SS officers. Their system, which functioned like an underground railroad, was dubbed the "Rat Line" by Americans.

The Rat Line took fugitives from Austria to Italy, where a Croatian priest, Father Krunoslav Dragonovic, handled the details of providing visas for various South American countries. Father Dragonovic was in charge of a seminary in Rome where Croatian youth studied for the priesthood. Because of Dragonovic's very important role, by 1948 this underground pipeline had already become known as the Monastery Route.

Hitler creates Croatia

In 1941 Hitler broke up Yugoslavia by creating the Independent State of Croatia. Zagreb became capital of this new country, and Anti Pavelic, a vicious anti-Serbian nationalist, assumed its leadership. Between 1941 and 1945, several hundred thousand Serbs were killed in Croatia; some 30,000 Jews were also brutally murdered.

When Hitler's Third Reich collapsed in 1945, the Independent State of Croatia collapsed with it. Yugoslavia was reunited under the leadership of Josef Tito, whose partisan guerilla movement had fought the Croatians during the war. Croatian leaders, fearing Tito's vengeance, scattered throughout Europe in the closing days of the war. Pavelic himself escaped to South America, with Father Dragonovic's assistance.

Father Dragonovic was known to our 430th CIC as a fascist and a war criminal. His connections with South American diplomats of similar backgrounds were generally met with disapproval by U.S. State Department officials.

Fr. Dragonovic enlists help of Church group

CIC normally gave its "travelers" Displaced Person status, and Father Dragonovic's link to the Catholic Church gave the Rat Line a respected front. It had even become known as the Vatican Connection after Father Dragonovic enlisted the services of the National Catholic Welfare Organization to help him secure the necessary travel permits for leaving Europe. CIC only had to bring the defectors to Genoa or Naples. Dragonovic took over from there.

CIC helped this priest perhaps inadvertently, spirit a number of war criminals wanted by the Allies out of Europe. In return, Father Dragonovic aided CIC when it had informants whose survival depended on leaving the continent. The Barbie family is a case in point. CIC paid Dragonovic from $1,000 to $1,400 for each adult defector he put into the pipeline; the amount was halved for children.

When, on December 11, 1950, CIC in Germany decided to send Barbie out of the country, they contacted CIC and the Intelligence Branch of U.S. Forces in Austria. In describing this contact, the technical specialist of CIC headquarters in Germany, filed the following report:

> *"a. The 430th CIC Detachment has been operating what they term a "Ratline" evacuation system to Central*

*and South America without serious repercussions
during the past three (3) years. At the cost of
approximately $1,000 each adult (U.S. legal tender)
430th CIC is transferring evacuees to Italy where
they are provided with legal documentation obtained
through devious means there. Overall supervision
and conduct of the operation is the sole responsibility
of Mr. NEAGOY, CIC Landsalzburg (sic). Actual
procurement of the documentation is handled by
the 430th's contact man in Italy.*

"*b. Representatives of the 430th CIC state that, if
necessary, they are prepared to undertake the
following action upon request. If an informant will
agree to emigrate to any available South or Central
American country, Mr. NEAGOY will visit this
headquarters to be briefed on the individual case and
interview the emigrant. Upon being provided with the
necessary funds, the 430th will assume responsibility
for transferring the individual to Italy and
arranging his emigration. The estimated time
requirement for completion of a case is six (6) to
sixteen (16) weeks.*"

On January 25, 1951, CIC requested approval from the
Intelligence Division of European Command to use the Rat
Line to dispose of Barbie. Travel documents were obtained
from the Combined Travel Board in Munich, and on
February 21 a temporary travel document—No. 0121455—
was issued to Klaus Altmann. A second document was
issued to Altmann's "wife and two children."

Barbie family smuggled to South America

On March 9, two CIC agents from Salzburg, Austria,
accompanied Barbie, his wife, and two children by train to
Salzburg. Two days later the family made their way to
Genoa, where they were housed in a hotel operated by
Father Dragonovic, who charged CIC $50 per day for each

adult. He obtained two very important documents for the Altmann family: an immigration visa to Bolivia, and a travel permit (in lieu of a passport) from the International Committee of the Red Cross.

A few days later an Argentinian transit visa was obtained and passage booked for the Barbie family on an Italian ship leaving Genoa for Buenos Aires, Argentina. Barbie and his family, under the name of Altmann, left Genoa on March 23 aboard the vessel Corrientes and arrived in Buenos Aires on April 10, 1951.

Once the "emigrants" had embarked, the 430th CIC was required to notify the State Department, through the Department of the Army, of their real and assumed names and provide personal data. The Department of State, in turn, would notify the United States Embassy or Consulate in the receiving country that the individuals in question were "formerly of interest to American Intelligence." Thus our State Department knew from the beginning that Barbie had become Altmann and moved with his family to Bolivia. France, meanwhile, continued to scour Europe for its most notorious war criminal. On April 3, CIC Headquarters commended everyone involved for the highly efficient manner in which the final disposal of an extremely sensitive individual had been handled. The memo concluded: "this case is considered closed by the Intelligence Division, European Command, and this Detachment."

Barbie becomes Bolivian businessman

Barbie's first contact in Bolivia was a former SS Colonel by the name of Frederich Schwendt. With Schwendt he got a job in a sawmill, later involving himself in such business enterprises as mining, the export-import trade, the sale of armaments, and trafficking in cocaine. In 1957 Barbie became a naturalized Bolivian citizen and was treated as a gentleman; in the traditional Latin manner he was referred

MINISTERIO DE TRANSPORTES D

D

Compañia Argentina de Navegación DODERO S. A.
BUENOS AIRES

BIGLIETTO D'IMBARCO IN TERZA CLASSE №. 15659
17/24-25

Sulla Nave di bandiera Argentina (*) ...CORRIENTES... in partenza

da **GENOVA** il ..22 MARZO 1951... per B. AIRES.... toccando di scalo i

port.NAPOLI - LAS PALMAS - RIO JANEIRO - SANTOS ... Durata del viaggio giorni ..O..

(compresa le fermate nei porti di scalo). - La durata del viaggio sarà aumentata di un giorno per ogni scalo eventuale.

COGNOME E NOME	ETÀ		POSTI e RAZIONI				Cuccette		EX	N.°
	Anni	Mesi	1	1/2	1/4	.0.	1	1/2		17489
									Prepagato	2863
1. ALTMANN KLANS	A	1					1		Buono ritorno	
2. " " MARIA	9		1					1	Ordinativo	
3.										
4.										

LLAMADA
Boleto N° TOTALE

(*) Caratteristiche della nave		
T..º CORRIENTES	N.... posti .... a posto	Compañia Argentina de Navegación
Stazza lorda T. 12851	Eccedenza posti	DODERO S. A.
netta T. 8633	a posto	Agenti Generali per l'Italia
Velocità alle	Supplemento cabina	DODERO -
prove miglia 17	Tasse	soc. per azioni
		Agenzie Marittime Argentine
	Totale	
	Acconto versato	
	Versato a saldo	
		Genova....

REGISTRAZIONE BAGAGLIO

Per il PASSEGGERO

180

to as Don Klaus. He made his services available to various Bolivian dictators in exchange for his own protection. He trained paramilitary troops and was appointed security advisor to former General and President of Bolivia Hugo Banzer, whose wife shared ownership of a large plantation with Barbie. His various business ventures fared well—providing him with villas in three Bolivian cities. His most lucrative undertaking proved to be the cocaine trade.

Some of Barbie's friends in Bolivia reportedly had connections with international terrorists. A man by the name of Joachim Fiebelkorn, according to German witnesses, arrived in Paraguay in 1977 and later went to Bolivia, where he met Barbie in Santa Cruz. Fiebelkorn is presently awaiting trial in Frankfurt, Germany, for allegedly participating in an attack on the railroad station in Bologna, Italy, in August, 1980, in which 85 people were killed. Tales of Barbie's years in exile abound with wild rumors and speculation. Many questions about his adventures as a *Boliviano* are expected to be answered at his trial.

By 1971 Klaus Barbie was half-forgotten. When he traveled on a Bolivian diplomatic passport to the United States, Germany, and France in 1969 and 1970, our Immigration and Naturalization Service took little notice. The court in Munich, Germany, that was handling litigation filed by some of Barbie's victims decided that it could take no action in their case.

On February 11, 1972, President Georges Pompidou of France sent a letter to President Banzer of Bolivia requesting Barbie's extradition. The request was denied. German-born Beate Klarsfeld organized demonstration after demonstration; her untiring efforts kept the Barbie case alive.

New government returns "Altmann" to France

In October, 1982, the new Bolivian government, under its present democratically elected president, Hernan Siles Zuazo, came into power. Bolivia then began to cooperate with the Mitterrand government of France. Instead of "extraditing" Barbie to France, the Bolivian government announced that it was "expelling" him. Because Bolivia has no extradition treaties, France and Germany offered Bolivia economic aid in exchange for Barbie.

The Butcher of Lyons was first symbolically held in Lyons' Montluc Prison, where he had tortured and murdured French Resistance Fighters. He now awaits his fate in Saint Joseph prison, in another part of the city. There are great debates in France about whether the death penalty should be reinstated in the Barbie case. Capital punishment was outlawed by the Mitterrand government. The French, however, can be expected to be meticulous in following the law so that there can be no suggestion that the trial was held to avenge Barbie's murder of French Resistance hero Jean Moulin.

Barbie was twice convicted in absentia of war crimes, and sentenced to death. But the time limit on these earlier convictions has expired, as the French statutes of limitation on all war crimes ran out after 20 years. Although he cannot be retried for the same crimes, he can be retried for acts against humanity, on which there are no time limitations.

Trial plans underway

Barbie is scheduled to be tried for eight specific charges of crimes against civilians. The murder of Resistance fighters falls under the category of war crimes and is thus inadmissible in Barbie's new trial of crimes against humanity. It was the judgment of the International Tribunal at Nürnberg that crimes against humanity were those carried out against the civilian population of a conquered country. If Barbie is found guilty of such crimes as deportation of Jews, execution of hostages, and assassination of civilians, his maximum sentence under current law would be life imprisonment.

Under no circumstances does France wish to be accused of a miscarriage of justice. The complex task of locating living witnesses will require the assistance of several countries, and in order to conform to the letter of the law, the preparation for Barbie's trial is expected to take more than a year. Experienced defense counsel has been appointed for Barbie by the government. His present lawyer, Jacques Verges, has made several unsuccessful attempts to have Barbie released on bond because of his irregular deportation from Bolivia to France.

To try Barbie on a handful of leftover crimes cannot do justice to Barbie's record, but it can begin the process of laying to rest the nightmare created by the Butcher of Lyons, and assuage some of the grief and pain felt by his victims' loved ones.

Barbie is under constant guard in his cell in Lyons. No visitors are allowed. His daughter, the only surviving member of his immediate family, has been allowed to visit him only once, after a minor hernia operation. Even investigators working on the Ryan Report, who had sought to interrogate Barbie in his cell, were denied permission to talk to him.

All indications are that the French handling of the trial will be impeccable. After all that has transpired, it would be tragic if deals were to be made or cover-ups engineered. All of France would like to be rid of the ghost that has been hanging over the country for almost forty years. By bringing to justice the man who brought such unprecedented suffering to her citizens, the trial can renew France's pride in the crucial role of the Resistance during the German occupation and its contribution to the country's final liberation.

*Photo of the author taken in October 1983
by Augsburger Allgemeine Zeitung, editor-
photographer, Alphons A. Schertl.*

Epilogue

We Americans normally repay our obligations. This was probably a major reason for the decision to help Barbie reach Bolivia. It would have been difficult to turn Barbie over to the French after he had spent four years working for the American Army. One good turn deserves another.

When my story of Barbie and the CIC connection in postwar Germany was made public, our government at first refused to investigate. Attorney General William French Smith, after being advised of the initial findings, ruled out further Justice Department action on the grounds that no prosecution was likely to result and that historical inquiry was not the job of his agency. At least ten members of the House of Representatives had appealed to President Reagan to investigate reports that Barbie had been protected after the war by American Intelligence Agencies. This was the beginning of the investigation that was to result in the Ryan Report. We now know that many CIC operators broke the law, but the Statute of Limitation on Obstruction of Justice is only five years in the United States. This five year period has long since expired, even if the presumed starting point is 1972, the year when France and the rest of the world learned that Klaus Altmann and Klaus Barbie were one and the same.

Because so many years have passed, it is easier today to forgive those overzealous CIC agents who took it upon themselves to use Barbie and hide him from the French. Most of those agents who are still living claim to have been unaware of Barbie's atrocities in France. This may possibly be true, since it appears that my reports about Barbie's atrocities were never made known to those who followed me. Many American agents believed crimes against French Resistance Fighters to have been acts of war. Some considered only the deportation of Jews a war crime and did not think that Barbie was guilty of that particular crime. But to believe that a chief of the SD special commando never deported Jews is an incredibly feeble excuse, an excuse that displays a total lack of knowledge of the Nazi regime.

It is true that the French were slow in initiating their investigations of German atrocities in Lyons in the postwar chaos of France. By the time we learned about Barbie's grisly past, he had been a valuable informant for over a year.

The excuse that the leadership of postwar France was riddled with communists is given considerable credence by the vote for the Constituent Assembly of October 21, 1945, which showed the communist party to have the largest electorate among the three major parties.

When Barbie names former collaborators during his trial, France will be forced to acknowledge the guilt of its own citizens during the Nazi era. Let us hope that France's re-examination of this episode of its past history does not unleash renewed animosity toward the German people. Since the end of the war, the world has demanded that Germans recognize their guilt during the Hitler regime;

Barbie's trial will demand the same introspection of France. France must both denounce her collaborators, of which there were once greater numbers than German occupation forces, and honor her Resistance heroes. Only then can the heavy burden of this ugly period of her history be lifted from her shoulders.

America seems to believe that it serves no purpose to prosecute Barbie after so much time has passed. Witnesses are dead and memories have become unsure. But Barbie's guilt can be proven by documents which he signed. Also, many former resistance fighters and other witnesses are still alive. We must not forget. The world must learn that atrocities do not belong in a civilized society. To allow ourselves to forget would be to admit our indifference, and would show an acceptance for the brutality of the Barbies of the world, wherever they may live.

The pre-trial investigations now underway indicate that Barbie will continue to lie. He claims he did nothing wrong. He maintains that he was not in Lyons at the time of the crimes for which he is being tried. If we adopt a complacent attitude because of the time that has elapsed, we will drift further from our European allies. France and Germany will lose more confidence in our ability to comprehend the feelings, aspirations, and culture, and history of our European friends. If we neglect to take a firm stand against Barbie simply on the grounds that brutality and torture are not uncommon in the world, we endanger our friendship with our allies in Europe. The friendship between France and Germany, which has finally been established on the basis of truth and trust, is especially vulnerable. The Friendship Treaty of January 1963, signed and sealed by Charles De Gaulle and Konrad Adenauer, is placed in jeopardy by the Barbie trial, if truth and honesty do not prevail.

For centuries, both countries had perpetuated the myth that the French and Germans were natural enemies from

time immemorial. Hate and distrust were taught in the
schools on both sides. Neither side emphasized that both
countries had a common founding father. The Emperor
Charlemagne was crowned on Christmas Day 800 A.D. and
ruled over the territories which would become France and
Germany. He was a leader of the Franks, a Germanic tribe.
The Germans referred to him as *Karl der Grosse* and his
major seat of power was in Aachen. To the French he was
Charlemagne of Aix-la-Chapelle (the French name for the
same city).

Allied cooperation with ex-Nazis has been well-
documented. The postwar actions of the Soviet Union were
much to blame for our employing men like Barbie. The cold
war and American inefficiency, rather than calculated
policy, were mitigating circumstances for use of former
Nazis. I deny that it was inevitable to seek the cooperation of
former Nazis. We should have been better prepared and
familiar with the reality of brutal systems like Hitlerism
and Stalinism. Not all governments persecute and torture
other people. The United States had no such policy during
and after the war. We must be honest, tell the truth, and not
look the other way, as many did after the war. If we do not
accept reality, we can justifiably ask the question: What has
mankind really learned from the brutality and killings of
World War II?

Memorandum from CIC Headquarters on various options how the U.S. may disassociate itself from Barbie.

HEADQUARTERS
66TH COUNTER INTELLIGENCE CORPS DETACHMENT
US ARMY, EUROPE

APO 154

MEMORANDUM TO COLONEL STEVENS

SUBJECT: Klaus BARBIE Case

1. Klaus BARBIE has been an informant of this organization since 1947, operating in the Region XII area. BARBIE was formerly a high official of Gestapo in LYON, France, and during his period of service is alleged to have tortured and killed many French patriots. Because of these alleged acts, BARBIE is wanted by the French for trial as a war criminal. Reference is made to Tab #1 which outlines the over-tures made by the French for the return of BARBIE to France for trial.

2. In January 1950, Region XII communicated with this headquarters and requested information as to the disposition of SUBJECT. By Minute 2, this headquarters ordered Region XII to maintain contact with SUBJECT; to keep him in the area; and to continue paying him from Confidential Funds, as it was necessary to have SUBJECT available in case the French desired to re-interrogate SUBJECT or to have SUBJECT extradited to France. (See Tab #2)

3. In April 1950, SUBJECT's name appeared on the German Police Want List. It was determined that the Surete had sponsored this request, and apparently had done so without clearance at a higher level, i.e., Surete contacted Wuerttemberg Police directly, contrary to existing regulations. Region XII at this time sent an IRS to this headquarters, which IRS was never answered. (See Tab #3)

Memo to Col STEVENS
Subject: Klaus BARBIE Case

4. In May 1950, Region XII S-3 sent an MOIC to this headquarters
again outlining the BARBIE case, together with possible ramifications.
The Regional Commander placed a 1st Indorsement to this MOIC approving
the S-3 comments. Region XII requested a decision coupled with guidance
from this headquarters in the BARBIE case but no information was
forwarded to Region XII either giving guidance or outlining the action
the region should take. (See Tab #4)

5. In May 1950, the HARDY treason trial started in PARIS. HARDY
was a member of the French Resistance and had given information to the
Gestapo - namely to BARBIE. The French wanted BARBIE as a witness
against HARDY - it is noted that the French papers stated the American
authorities refused to allow BARBIE to appear as a witness. The truth
is that the French did not make a proper request, and that Lieutenant
WHITEWAY of BDOC was the initial party to ask for BARBIE's appearance
as a material witness. When WHITEWAY discovered that the French would
not return BARBIE to Germany, WHITEWAY withdrew his request. No
additional requests were made at that time. It is pointed out that
apparently two factions in France are involved in a political manuever.
The Communists want BARBIE to return , while other factions would prefer
to have him remain in Germany. The latter faction have good reason, as
many influential Frenchman, who presently hold high positions, were
interrogated by BARBIE during the early days of the occupation of France.
For example, PONCET and LaBRUN(PONCET, I believe, is presently High
Commissioner in Germany). Note Tab #5 which indicates the unfavorable
publicity on this matter which was forwarded by letter to General TAYLOR.

-2-

Memo to Col STEVENS
Subject: Klaus BARBIE Case

6. On the 18th of May, 1950, a TWX was received from Major COLLINS, ID, indicating that the German police were looking for BARBIE, and had requested the cooperation of this detachment. No action is indicated. (See Tab #6)

7. On 21 August 1950, a SRI was received from ID requesting the extradition of BARBIE. This SRI was replied to by letter this headquarters, dated 30 August, which stated that this headquarters was complying with original decision made in May 1950. The decision referred to is notated on Tab #1 and indicates that Colonels ERSKINE, ECKMANN, LIGON and JOHNSON, Majors WILSON and DANIELS, and Mr. VIDAL agreed that BARBIE should not be placed in the hands of the French. (See Tab #7)

8. The most current document in SUBJECT's dossier is a TWX from ID, dated 9 September 1950, which indicates that Colonel ERSKINE had informed I.D. that this headquarters has no objection to the extradition of SUBJECT. A Memo for Record indicates that Colonel HARDICK, I.D., was informed that we are no longer connected with BARBIE, and therefore, have no objection to the extradition. No other explanation is given for the reversal of decision. (See Tab #8)

9. A problem is therefore presented in view of the above decision. Region XII is still harboring SUBJECT and his family in a Liaison House, and is not only supporting SUBJECT, but is utilizing him as an informant. Region XII is acting properly under orders of this headquarters inasmuch as the region was informed in January 1950 to keep SUBJECT on the payroll. Region XII has pointed out to this headquarters on several occasions

REGRADED UNCLASSIFIED
ON 21 JUL 1983

193

Memo to Col STEVENS
Subject: Klaus BARBIE Case

since that date the problem involved and has requested guidance but
no definite action has been taken by this headquarters thus far to
alleviate Region XII's problem.

10. During recent discussions with Region XII representatives,
the BARBIE case again came to the attention of this section and Major
RUSSI in turn ordered a review of the dossier as outlined above for
further consideration at this time by Colonel STEVENS.

11. RECOMMENDATIONS: It is deemed important that this organization immediately disassociate itself with BARBIE. If this action had
been taken a year ago, a time cushion would by now have been employed
to our advantage and would have somewhat minimized any possible
repercussions to this unit. Undoubtedly, Colonel ERSKINE's decision
to allow I.D. to have SUBJECT extradited must have been founded on a
strong basis, which is however not indicated in the written record.
(It is presumed that Colonel ERSKINE believed the implications of Tab
#8 to this memo be carried through.) However, it is pointed out that
SUBJECT, if extradited, is still in a position to:

a. cause a great deal of adverse publicity to CIC in particular
and to the Armed Forces in general. In short, in order to vindicate
himself, BARBIE will point out that he has served CIC faithfully against
Communism for the past several years; this in turn, will expose the
fact that this detachment failed initially to arrest him as an automatic
arrestee, later failed to turn him over to the British who also wanted
him; this unit has probably used the services of a war criminal and
protected such person from legal authority.

Memo to Col STEVENS
Subject: Klaus BARBIE Case

b. expose this organizations modus operandi, many KEI's, and
compromise sensitive penetration informants who are still active in the
AUGSBURG area.

c. point out the names of several unsavory "personalities"
that have been protected and employed by CIC.

In reality, BARBIE was "pressed" into service by this organization when
he was arrested for having been associated with an SS underground movement.
BARBIE at that time was made to swear that he would sever connections
with the SS movement and serve this organization. To date SUBJECT has
fulfilled his portion of the contract and has apparently served this
organization well. The following plan of action is proposed:

PLAN

(1) This organization completely and with all finality sever all
relations with SUBJECT. It must be pointed out firmly to SUBJECT that
he has no alternative but to adhere to our desires, as his life is at
stake as well as his future security.

(2) SUBJECT must be given a debriefing payment in order to enable
both he and his family (wife and two children) to be financially
independent until absorbed and lost in the German economy.

(3) This unit may then either:

(a) passively assist SUBJECT in processing himself through
several refugee camps as an Illegal Border Crosser in order to enable
him to obtain legal documentation and that way completely lose his
identity, or

-5-

195

Memo to Col STEVENS
Subject: Klaus BARBIE Case

(b) Inform SUBJECT that this unit no longer desires him to
remain in the AUGSBURG area because the French are exerting pressure
in their search for him. Also inform him that this headquarters will
no longer protect him from the French and that he is completely on
his own, to do what he pleases.

By following plan (a), it is noted that we will be assured that SUBJECT
will completely lose his identity. CIC need not even appear on the
scene, other than to watch the developments from the side-lines. However, by following plan (b), in addition to disassociating ourselves
with SUBJECT we would also be able to preclude any possible further
tie-in with SUBJECT. It is pointed out that SUBJECT has on two occasions escaped from the British and on one accasion escaped from the
American authorities. SUBJECT is a professional intelligence man who
is very capable and qualified to take care of himself - unless this organization
persists in remaining his guardian angel.

13. Recent conference with Region XII indicates that SUBJECT is
very cooperative in his frame of mind and is willing to follow any
procedure set forth by this organization inasmuch as he is living in
constant fear of being apprehended by the French.

14. It is believed that if SUBJECT is disassociated with this
organization, given a debriefing sum to rehabilitate himself, it is
not believed that he will be apprehended in the near future by either
the allied or German authorities. Further, based upon past experience,
it is believed that the moment the German government receives a portion
of its authority under the "technical peace" the function now performed

-6-

GRADED UNCLASSIFIED

1-R

196

Memo to Col STEVENS
Subject: Klaus BARBIE Case

by the "Extradition Commission" of the Allied High Commissioners Office

will become a function of the German government.   BARBIE obviously is

still a patriot to the German government.

W. J. UNRATH
Captain, Artillery
Technical Specialist Section

History of the Rat Line as reported by
Headquarters of U.S. Forces in Austria.

Informal Routing Slip

Hq. Operations
D[ ] 113 9   A

HEADQUARTERS
UNITED STATES FORCES IN AUSTRIA

#1751
198-14

SUBJECT: History of the Italian Rat Line

Number each message consecutively. Fill in all columns, authenticate message,
draw a line across the page just below authentication. Use entire width of
page. Use only for inter-office communication:

NO.	FROM	TO	DATE	MESSAGE
1	Hq 430th CIC Opns	D/G-2 ATTN: Maj Milano	10 Apr 50	**1. ORIGINS.**

1. ORIGINS.

a. During the summer of 1947 the undersigned received instructions from G-2, USFA, through Chief CIC, to establish a means of disposition for visitors who had been in the custody of the 430th CIC and completely processed in accordance with current directives and requirements, and whose continued residence in Austria constituted a security threat as well as a source of possible embarrassment to the Commanding General of USFA, since the Soviet Command had become aware of their presence in US Zone of Austria and in some instances had requested the return of these persons to Soviet custody.

b. The undersigned, therefore, proceeded to Rome where, through a mutual acquaintance, he conferred with a former Slovakian diplomat who in turn was able to recruit the services of a Croation Roman Catholic Priest, Father Dragonivich. Father Dragonivich had by this time developed several clandestine evacuation channels to the various South American countries for various types of European refugees.

2. HISTORY OF OPERATIONS.

a. During 1947 and 1948 it was necessary to escort the visitors physically from Austria to Rome from the standpoint of security and to avoid any embarrassment on the part of the US Government which could arise from faulty documentation or unforeseen border and police incidents.

b. Documents to assist in the journey of these people from Austria to Rome were secured through S/A Crawford, Reference IRS, Subject: "Debriefing of S/A Crawford", dated 6 April 1950.

c. Upon arrival in Rome, the visitors were turned over to Dragonivich who placed them in safe haven houses being operated under his direct supervision. During this period, the undersigned then actively assisted Father Dragonivich with the help of a US citizen, who was Chief of the eligibility office of IRO in Rome, in securing additional documentation and IRO aid for further transportation. This, of course, was done illegally

~~TOP SECRET~~

D/G-2 TS REG No. 3 3 3
COPY No. 1

Informal Routing Slip

HEADQUARTERS
UNITED STATES FORCES IN AUSTRIA

Hq Operations
1139

#1751
198-14

SUBJECT: History of the Italian Rat Line (Minute 1 Continued)

Number each message consecutively. Fill in all columns, authenticate message,
draw a line across the page just below authentication. Use entire width of
page. Use only for inter-office communication:

NO.	FROM	TO	DATE	MESSAGE

inasmuch as such persons could not possibly qualify for eligibility under the
Geneva IRO Charter. However, after several months the American suddenly lost
his mental stability through overindulgence in alcohol and disclosed some of
the details of the arrangement to his superiors and other official agencies in
Rome which required the undersigned to realign the operation and to discontinue
contact with the IRO office. Thus, Father Dragonivich was forced to turn to
other sources in the National Catholic Welfare Organization. He also secured
permits for residence of these persons from the Italian police, permits to
travel from Rome to Genoa or Naples, as the case might be, and permits from the
Italian Foreign Office for various visas. In short, it can be stated that
Dragonivich handled all phases of the operation after the defectees arrived in
Rome, such as the procurement of IRO Italian and South American documents, visas,
stamps, arrangements for disposition, land or sea, and notification of resettlement committees in foreign lands.

     d. As the operation continued,
Dragonivich's possibilities for the necessary means, documentation, travel and
permits expanded and it became possible to ship the visitors from Austria, thus
eliminating personal escort by CIC agents to Rome. A new phase was thus established and an employee of Dragonivich proceeded to Austria, picked up the charges
and took them to Genoa where they were placed in safe haven houses to await disposition to South America.

    3. DIFFICULTIES ENCOUNTERED.

     The following difficulties
and problems may be expected by those who may become engaged in rat line operations:

     a. Frequent changes in travel
documents necessary for movement in European countries.

     b. Changes in the Italian
border control and police supervision of DP's in Italy.

     c. Land and sea transporta-
tion facilities or lack thereof.

TOP SECRET

478

HEADQUARTERS
UNITED STATES FORCES IN AUSTRIA

SUBJECT: History of the Italian Rat Line (Minute 1 Continued)

Number each message consecutively. Fill in all columns, authenticate message,
draw a line across the page just below authentication. Use entire width of
page. Use only for inter-office communication:

NO.	FROM	TO	DATE	MESSAGE

d. Opening and closing of
immigration quotas by the various countries of South America.

e. The physical condition of
visitors and dependents. It may be stated here that it is desirable that all
persons be examined for TB, syphilis or other contagious diseases and that the
female dependents be cautioned during the evacuation period relative to preg-
nancy, inasmuch as pregnant women or small children are acceptable only with
grave difficulty and at great expense.

f. Marriage Status. In view
of the fact that Dragonivich is a Roman Catholic priest and the National
Catholic Welfare is involved, the marriage status of male and female must be
clearly established, inasmuch as the personalities associated in this operation
will not condone any acts contrary to the Church such as common law marriage,
illegitimate children not baptized, etc.

g. Although it might be ad-
vantageous to have absolute "control" of Father Dragonivich and his means of
evacuation, it may be categorically stated that it is not possible and in the
opinion of the undersigned not entirely desirable. Dragonivich is known and
recorded as a Fascist, war criminal, etc., and his contacts with South American
diplomats of a similar class are not generally approved by US State Department
officials, plus the fact that in the light of security, it is better that we may
be able to state, if forced, that the turning over of a DP to a Welfare Organization falls in line with our democratic way of thinking and that we are not engaged in illegal disposition of war criminals, defectees and the like.

4. COMPROMISES.

a. As stated above, the US
citizen, Chief of the Eligibility Office, Rome, was one ▮▮▮▮▮▮▮▮ who
was allegedly a member of OSS during World War II, and who fancied himself as
a top intelligence operative in Italy. After his breakdown due to alcoholism,
▮▮▮▮▮ imagined himself as the saviour of Italy in view of the danger of a
Communist victory during the elections of 1948, thus told stores of how the

~~TOP SECRET~~

REGRADED UNCLASSIFIED
ON   21 JUL 1983
BY CDR USAINSCOM FOIPO
Auth Para 1-603 DoD 5200.1-R

#1751
198-14

SUBJECT: History of the Italian Rat Line (Minute 1 Continued)

Number each message consecutively. Fill in all columns, authenticate message, draw a line across the page just below authentication. Use entire width of page. Use only for inter-office communication:

NO.	FROM	TO	DATE	MESSAGE

undersigned could assist in providing large numbers of underground troops, military supplies, sea evacuation, air evacuation and the like. This, of course, caused inquiries as to the exact nature of the work in which the undersigned was engaged. This was explained away successfully in a personal interview with Admiral Mentz, Chief of IRO, Italy, and a full report was submitted to G-2, USFA.

b. The Brazil Expedition was, again, a compromise which was not the fault of operational technique. A female visitor who was inclined to be rather frivolous in her attentions became a public nuisance while under protective custody in Austria and was, therefore, evacuated as a married woman in custody of her amour of the moment. During the voyage, the lady in question changed her mind and upon arrival in Brazil sought assistance and protection from both the Brazilian authorities and the US Embassy. They, of course, were uninformed, inasmuch as it is impossible, due to lack of knowledge of transportation dates, visa quotas, etc., to give prior information as to when the shipments are to be made. The affair was made a matter of official investigation and necessarily other innocent people were involved and returned to Europe.

5. RECOMMENDATIONS.

a. It has been the experience of this organization that only one man should be assigned the mission of disposition when dealing with Father Dragonivich. Inasmuch as he, although reliable from a security standpoint, is unscrupulous in his dealings concerning money, as he does a considerable amount of charity work for which he receives no compensation, it is not entirely impossible that he will delay one shipment for one organization to benefit another organization who pays higher prices.

b. Due to the background of Father Dragonivich and the nature of his work, it is not believed practical that the MA's in foreign countries under diplomatic status should become involved with the DP's who land through his channels of this operation.

c. Each visitor should be thoroughly and properly briefed and preparations for his movement be made in the light of his cover story. Each should be furnished sufficient clothing, some

TOP SECRET

Informal Routing Slip

SUBJECT: **History of the Italian Rat Line (Minute 1 Continued)**

Number each message consecutively. Fill in all columns, authenticate message,
draw a line across the page just below authentication. Use entire width of
page. Use only for inter-office communication:

NO.	FROM	TO	DATE	MESSAGE

travel money, and advance notice be sent through Dragonivich channels to assist
in his rehabilitation in the country where he lands.

        d. The facilities of Father
Dragonivich should be handled as a single operation by one agency and no attempt
should be made to control him or his sources for reasons set forth in this
memorandum.

FOR THE COMMANDING OFFICER:

PAUL E LYON
IB Operations Officer

Tel: Salzburg 1146

Copy No. 2 burned
14/4/50 - RW.

REGRADED UNCLASSIFIED
ON **21 JUL 1983**
BY CDR USAINSCOM FOIPO
Auth Para 1-603 DoD 5200.1-R

TOP SEC

205